Parkstone

A history of its golf club

L C Jenkins

PARKSTONE GOLF CLUB

ISBN 0 9512354 0 0

Printed in England by
Roman Press Limited, Bournemouth.

Contents

Acknowledgements

Book jacket — *Water colour by David Sque*

Photographs of modern course — *Dr. J H Bailey*

Views of old course — *Supplied by Andrew Hawkes*

Photographs of presentations in clubhouse — *Major H Munro*

It is difficult to realise that (this is) but a recent evolution from wild moorland. In this year of grace 1939 I am impelled to carry my memory back over at least half a century, when with my brothers I was wont to chase the elusive lizard and butterfly over this self-same spot ...... Not a house was to be seen save Brownsea Castle nestling among its green trees, the summer air laden with those exquisite scents that go with heather, bracken and pine.

Ben Boothby, creator of Compton Acres gardens.

Foreword

WITH SCANT REGARD for the relative topography, early nineteenth century residents lauded Parkstone as the Mentone of the South, and it was to this fashionable, beautiful and aristocratic suburb that the more exalted residents of Poole moved as the old town spilled over its boundaries.

There were admittedly a few artisans working at the local pottery, but generally the tree-clad hills provided healthy sunny slopes for the villa residences of retired officers of the Crimean and colonial wars, delicate ladies, and retired businessmen.

The Parkstone of today is still a beautiful place in which to live, and its wooded hills still shelter many villas of the successful, but too many are scarred by multi-storied flats, and old delightful arbors have disappeared to make room for the increasing influx of new residents.

However, one completely unspoiled area remains to delight the heart of visitor and resident alike: over the years the title of the Parkstone and Canford Cliffs Golf Links has been shortened to exclude Canford, and the course has changed from its sandy links character to heather-edged parkland winding through pine woods which have been beautified by the addition of Rhododendron and deciduous flowering trees and shrubs.

Parkstone remains in the postal district of Poole, but in the mind of the majority of its summer visitors the course is probably more closely associated with Bournemouth. Certainly the early advertisements for the club highlighted its proximity to the seaside resort, which was steadily increasing in popularity, and which itself included the courses at Broadstone and Ferndown in its own list of attractions.

There is therefore throughout this history a dichotomy of association, especially for the early period, because so much of the information came from archive copies of the *Bournemouth Echo*.

There are three distinct phases in the club's history: beginning in 1910 and for the first seventeen years it was a private club owned by Lord Wimborne; it was then bought by six local businessmen and run as a proprietary club for thirty-three years; in 1961 it became a members' club.

No records exist for the time the club was in private hands so it has been necessary to rely for contemporary accounts of its activities on local newspapers and golf journals. For information on the second phase grateful acknowledgement is due to J R Stutt who was responsible for executing the re-design of the course in 1933 and who returned to become in turn a member of the club, a major shareholder, Chairman of the Board of Directors, and ultimately President of the members' club. He retained the minute books of the meetings of the Directors and kindly made them available for study. Many thanks are also due to J Hamilton Stutt who, since his father's retirement, has been responsible for many improvements to the course. As a long-standing member of the club and a well-known golf course architect, he is uniquely qualified to provide much of the information for the chapter dealing with the evolution of the course.

Many valuable papers dealing with the early part of the period of members' ownership were lost due to a burglary at the clubhouse in 1976 and the secretary of the day, although a true gentleman and one of the most popular members in the recent history of the club, was not renowned for efficient paperkeeping, so again it has been necessary to rely on external sources for information about that period.

A plan which shows the two main layouts of the golf course should be folded-out from the back of the book to assist the reader to identify the areas being described in the text.

The original course designed by Willie Park in 1910, together with the land which was then encompassed is shown in red, and superimposed is the major re-design carried out by James Braid following the purchase of the marshland from Lord Alington in 1932, and this is fundamentally the layout which exists today. There have been numerous modifications to both layouts, but these have been mainly of a cosmetic nature and many have been short-lived. The two courses shown on the plan are therefore as accurate as the available records will permit them to be drawn.

L C J

1 *Benevolent patronage 1910 to 1927*

1 *Benevolent patronage 1910 to 1927*

A WILDERNESS OF TREES AND HEATHER is how a local journalist described this part of the Canford estate in 1910 when Lord Wimborne bought the reservoirs and land from the Poole Water Company and set about transforming the area into a golf course.

It was said at the time that the noble lord was more interested in enhancing the value of the land than in creating an amenity, but be that as it may, his industry and enterprise added another jewel to the necklace of islands which encircle the old harbour and one which has provided pleasure for thousands of visitors and local golfers.

Willie Park junior, son of the winner of the first Open, and himself twice winner of the title, was commissioned to design the layout, and in his report to his Lordship's agents he visualised *a first-class course, fit for championship matches, which will, because of its natural undulating formation, give the sporting character essential to high class golf, and will rank in the front line of English golf courses.*

Work began on the construction of the course in June 1909, beginning at the Parkstone end of the Luscombe valley and running in a southerly direction through the Compton Acre. Two hundred and fifty workmen transformed the wilderness into an embryo golf course within five months, and it was ready for play eleven months after the work began.

The same local journalist observed *it is possible that Mr Willie Park has been responsible for more golf courses than any other man in England, and it is satisfactory to know that he is eminently satisfied with*

Parkstone. The eighteen holes measure close on to six thousand yards, and affords a thoroughly good test of all-round golf. It is a distinctly sporting course, by no means easy, as the natural lie of the land lends itself admirably to the purpose. Mr Park has certainly made the most of his opportunities. He has utilised the reservoirs twice, once for the drive on the third, and again for a chip onto the sixth. All the greens are exceptionally well guarded with bunkers. In fact the concensus of opinion seems to be that the course will be one of the best in the South of England.

In spite of this glowing description Willie Park's layout fell far short of the ideal and he was not able to make the best use of the natural facilities. The course was unbalanced, with eleven par fours; rather shorter than it could have been and with too many blind holes. In addition many of the holes were grouped too closely together which called for much circumspection when playing around about the eighth, ninth and tenth. The reservoirs did not feature in the layout as can be seen from the fold-out map of the course, and were not incorporated into the course layout until a tee was constructed between the lakes on the recommendation of Hamilton Stutt in the 1970s.

A suggestion as to the reason for excluding this very obvious feature is contained in the chapter which deals in detail with the evolution of the course, but whatever the shortcomings of the original design, the course attracted many fine players and much favourable comment from the visitors to Bournemouth who were surprised to find such a high class golf club so close to a select holiday town which was steadily growing in popularity.

An extract from the 1911 issue of *Nisbet's Golf Annual* shows that visitors were directed to the course via the nearby railway station or by the tram service.

PARKSTONE G C Instituted 1910. Tram to Bournemouth (16 minutes). Station Parkstone, ¾ mile; Poole 2 miles. Number of members 250. Hon Sec Major C J U Morris, Rossenara, West Cliff, Bournemouth. Entrance fee 3 gns. 18 holes. Pro: H Williamson. Green fees 2/6d per day and 12/6d per week.

The course overlooks Poole harbour. The greens are good and the holes have plenty of variety. Subsoil sandy. By arrangement with the Royal Dorset G C at Broadstone, members for a joint fee of 4 gns and subs of 4 gns. Will have the choice of 2 full-length courses less than five miles apart with a good train service. The Bournemouth courses are also quite close. 2d. tram from Bournemouth.

No records exist for the first seventeen years of the club's life, so it has been necessary to rely on information gleaned from local newspapers. Unfortunately golf reporting was very erratic, ranking a very poor third to cricket and football in spite of the fact that Bournemouth was the first local authority in England to provide municipal golf links, consequently details of the many interesting events which took place in those early years have been lost forever.

The first committee, formed in 1909, consisted of Lord Wimborne as President; Captain the Right Honourable F E Guest as Chairman, and Major C J U Morris as Vice Chairman; with Colonel R H Walter, F G Wheatley, Dr Paterson, T Meek and A F Fellowes. Mr G Chapman of Stanley Green Poole was listed as Secretary, but it can be assumed that he only looked after the internal affairs of the club because Major Morris' name was the only one which featured in subsequent reports.

This committee nominated the first one hundred members and thirty ladies whose position at that time was not defined, but they had no say in the running of the club. Each of these original members was entitled to nominate one other person for membership subject to the approval of the committee. The list was closed on the first day of January 1910 and from that date the entrance of two guineas, plus two guineas subscription, was raised to three guineas.

It is a great pity that no records exist for the period around the opening of the club because it would be interesting to discover why or how the decision was taken to engage a professional from as far away as Nottinghamshire. Admittedly Dorset was a relatively barren area with regard to golf, but there would have been plenty to choose from in the Southern and Home counties. In the event Hugh Williamson the professional at Longcliffe, then known as the Nanpanton Golf Club, was appointed, and the local paper of the period mentioned Padley who served as his assistant until Edmund, the younger of the three Williamsons, joined him in 1913.

Professionals in those days were quite literally servants of the club members, they were engaged primarily for their clubmaking ability. Williamson's contract has not survived because Lord Wimborne's papers which dealt with the details of the golf club were destroyed by fire when Liverpool was bombed during the war. However, the letter of appointment which the Notts Golf Club sent to Hugh's brother Tom is a typical job description, and it is reasonable to suppose that Hugh was expected to provide similar services for the retired senior officers and gentlemen who formed the majority of the membership of the new club.

The Committee ... instruct me to say that they are willing to engage you temporarily as clubmaker etc. on the following terms:-

1 That you shall be at the service (so far as your other duties will permit) of any member of the club to play with him or coach him at a charge of 1s.6d. a round (18 holes) including caddie; same charge to apply to a round of the Ladies Links, whether with a member of the club or the ladies club.

2 That you should take charge of the Clubhouse and be responsible for its safety.

3 That you should take the management of the caddies and the caddies' shelter.

4 That you should conduct the draw on Medal days.

5 That you should assist in keeping the course and greens in order, giving your services upon them for eight hours a week, these hours to be given on such days and at such times as the Committee, or the Greenkeeper on their behalf may require.

6 That you may receive from the club 5/- a week.

7 That you should take all profits from making, mending and selling clubs and balls.

8 That this engagement may be determined at any time by fourteen days' notice on either side.

I want to make it quite clear that the engagement is temporary. Of course it may eventually become of a more permanent nature, but for the present you must be good enough to understand that it is only temporary and experimental, and the Committee will feel themselves at liberty to determine it at any time on giving the above notice.

Tom Williamson spent the whole of his professional career with the Notts club, but his contract was never confirmed.

Play was permitted on the Parkstone course for the first time in May 1910 and the club was officially opened later in that same year. In addition to it being Bournemouth's centenary year, with all its attendant celebrations, 1910 was a particularly good year for news, so that not a single mention of the Parkstone opening appeared in any of the local papers.

This is perhaps not surprising because the small matter of the opening of a new golf course could not possibly compete with the visit of the Lord Mayor of London, complete with state coach; aeroplane races and demonstration flights (one of which resulted in the death of C S Rolls); the death of King Edward VII and the coronation of King George V; plus of course the historic pursuit and capture of the notorious Dr Crippen; truly a bonanza year for a small provincial newspaper.

The club was not out of the news for long however because within the very first year of its existence it created legal history by taking to Court an appeal against the tax assessment. The reports of the hearings brought to light some very interesting details of the costs of constructing and running a golf club in those days.

The appeal was heard at the Poole Quarterly Sessions in July 1911. The club contended that the gross assessment was *far in excess of the rental if the property was let from year to year* and that *the present expenditure was far in excess of receipts.* The Court was asked to decide whether a golf course ought to be regarded as having monopoly value and its rating based upon profit-earning capacity, or whether the basis should be the amount spent for reconstruction purposes.

The clubhouse in its original 1911 setting. The 18th green has now disappeared beneath the bungalows beside what is now Links Road.

The report revealed that the cost of constructing the golf course was £8,660, which included £7,000 for laying it out, and in addition the clubhouse cost £2,500 to build.

The rateable value of the course was assessed at £550 gross and £440 net, and the total area was seventy-one acres of which fifty-three were grassed. Total membership was 262, including eighty ladies. Income in the first year was £528, and the loss £800. The cost of the upkeep apart from development was £1,231 and the expected expenditure for 1911 was £1400, compared to the expected income of £900. Major Morris, acting for the golf club, told the Sessions that the estimated cost of maintaining the course when the development was complete would be £900 per annum, and that the estimated total membership would be 280 gentlemen (no mention of ladies). He also claimed that the club would never pay its way, *when the club settled down they hoped for an income of £1,050 and an expenditure of £900, being a balance of £150.*

The Assessors estimated the value of the land at £200 an acre and the rating was assessed at £3 an acre. The £7,000 spent on the course, put at 4%, gave £280, and £2,500 for the club-house at 5%, gave £125. The Assessment Committee then made a substantial reduction down to £550 gross and £440 net. By way of comparison the Assessors stated that the Broadstone course was rated at £450 gross and £320 net.

The Recorder postponed a decision on the appeal until the next Sessions so that he could view the course. This he subsequently did and at the next sitting the rates were reduced, but not by the hoped-for amount.

The report of the appeal, which was published in the *Bournemouth Echo,* contained a number of interesting observations. The Recorder discussed the appeal at some length, from the viewpoint of a hypothetical landlord and a hypothetical tenant, alluding to the idea of a person or a syndicate acquiring such a property for the purpose of speculation, and to run a club in the hope of making a profit. He observed that it would be quite possible that some landowner with building land ripe for development in the neighbourhood might find it worthwhile to run a golf club either for a monetary purpose, or for adding to the amenities of the neighbourhood and raising the value of the surrounding building land. He observed that if the figures were accepted as being totally reliable no golf club could afford more than about £150 in rent, but came to the conclusion that the links would not be let at such a low figure. In his opinion the club would be able, either by increasing the fees, or membership, or both, to pay a considerably larger sum than £150.

With regard to the contention that the rating should be accorded to the amount spent on reconstruction and the likely return if looked upon as a commercial undertaking, the Recorder came to the conclusion that the course was laid out by Lord Wimborne without any idea of making it pay as a club, but for the very natural and legitimate object of adding to the amenities of the neighbourhood and increasing and developing the value of his other land.

As to the value of the land as it stood and its respective building land, an expert assessed it at £150 an acre, and this would make the total value of the land alone as £10,000 and upward, justifying the original tax estimate. He felt however that he had to think of it as a golf links and not as building land. By comparison, although the rateable value of the Broadstone links was lower, it was comparatively *out in the country* and the land there was presumably of less value as building land.

The green fees at Broadstone were 2/6d a day, whereas at Parkstone they were three shillings. Major Morris interjected to say that the fees had been placed deliberately high to guard against a rush of players.

The Parkstone links were situated in a growing residential district and whilst anyone would admit that the Broadstone links were very superior, it might be that many persons would be prepared to give a good subscription to get golf practically at their door and thus save the railway journey to Broadstone.

At the previous hearing it was stated that a syndicate had offered to rent the links from Lord Wimborne at an annual rent of £400, but the offer was withdrawn when it was ascertained that Sunday golf would not be permitted.

The Recorder finally agreed that the rate fixed by the Assessment Committee was too high and reduced it to £454 gross and £350 net, a reduction of £90.

Early play

The first open meeting at the club was held on Thursday October 26 1911 and the *Bournemouth Echo* reported that *so assiduous has been the attention paid by Hope the Greenkeeper to the course, which is a full one of eighteen holes, that visitors have expressed a great satisfaction that the greens are in such splendid condition; one player remarking that there was not a weed to be seen.*

It would appear that the meeting lasted longer than one day because the reporter referred to the programme for the Thursday being devoted to a bogey sweep and two other competitions. The bogey for the course was 78, and the winner was E P A Day, all square, and the runner-up D C Greenlees, two down. There were thirty-eight entries for the Original Members Cup which was played for under handicap over eighteen holes. The other trophies played for were the Cecil Cup, the Wimborne Cup and the Challenge Cup, which were to be held for one year. The membership was quoted as being 185 *and increasing rapidly.*

The following month, on the eighth, the ladies held their first meeting. *The arrangements were made by a committee consisting of Mrs Bevan (Capt), Mrs Fellowes, Miss Pontifex, Miss Frye and Miss Carroll. A considerable quantity of rain fell until about ten o'clock and the greens were somewhat heavy, but most of the play took place in fine weather, although a boisterous wind prevailed.*

The chief competition was for the Challenge Bowl presented by Lady Wimborne and played over eighteen holes under handicap. It was won by Mrs Doig (12) with a net 86. In the approach and putt competition the best score (9) was by Miss Fowler, Miss Mills came second with 10 after a tie with three others. The driving competition (best of three) was won by Miss Carroll who reached 163 yards with the ball against the wind.

Details of occurrences up to the time of the transfer of ownership are sketchy, but the local paper for July 11th 1912 carried the report of a qualifying competition played over the course by the western section of the PGA for the £400 *News of the World* tournament. The qualifiers were E R Whitcombe of Came Down (71, 73, = 144), and E Foord of Burnham and Berrow (74, 74, = 148).

Whitcombe's morning round of 71 established a record for the course which was to stand until 1923 when Hugh Williamson cut it to 65, a record which was not equalled or bettered over the original course. Capt R E Wemyss set the amateur record with a 71 in an open scratch contest for the Wimborne Cup in October 1913. Hugh Williamson also recorded the first hole-in-one on the course when he holed his tee shot at the eighth. What a prodigious feat this would have been today, because instead of his little 107 yard knock, he would have to have driven a curling 334 yard shot into a green which is practically surrounded by trees and bunkers.

There is of course the technical advancement in golf equipment to consider, but even in those days there was a great deal of discussion about the length the professionals could drive a golf ball. A demonstration was held at the Sandy Lodge Golf Club in Hertfordshire in 1919 in an effort to disprove the popular belief that first-class golfers could drive the ball impossible distances. Four of the best-known golfers of the day, Vardon, Braid, Taylor and Alec Herd, took part and in near-perfect conditions the longest drive was 257 yards, and the best average was Braid's 213 yards.

The R & A were of the opinion that the power of the ball should be limited in order to retain the special features of the game and to preserve a balance in relation to the length of the holes. After consultation with American, Canadian and South

Hugh Williamson, still wearing his 'breeks' and cap, relaxing at his beach hut in Branksome. The over-dressed gentleman on the left is his nephew, the young Tom Williamson. The lady is Hugh's second wife with her son Jackie and their son who was nicknamed 'Bubbles'.

African golfing authorities, the R & A agreed on a standard ball which became known as the '30', a fraction lighter and smaller than the most popular ball of the day. An extract from the notes on the resolution, kindly supplied by the Historian of the R & A throws some light on the differences of opinion which existed between the British and the American authorities at the time (1912).

.... the first rubber cored ball, the Haskell was a light floating ball of a size equal to a gutta ball of from 27 to 27½ dwts. The elasticity of the present ball has not materially increased, but the ball, being much smaller, offers less resistance to the wind, and being much heavier does not require the same skill for its control.... On hard ground the distances obtained do away with the various strokes made by wooden clubs through the green which were formerly characteristic features of the game. On soft ground little skill is required in pitching, for the ball breaks the upper crust of the putting green and after making a hole or burying itself, remains where it falls. Under these circumstances the pitch and run shot is no longer required. From the point of view of the golf courses these small heavy balls are destructive. They lie so close to the ground that turf is now nearly always taken in making a stroke through the green; even on the teeing ground of a short hole professionals, and some amateurs, instead of taking a tee put the ball in a hole and take a divot.

This decision remained in force until changed by a conference between the two committees in Muirfield in June 1920, when it was decided *that the weight of the ball shall not be greater than 1.62 ounces and the size not less than 1.62 inches in diameter. The Rules of Golf Committee and the Executive Committee of the United States Golf Association will take whatever steps they think necessary to limit the power of the ball with regard to distance, should any ball of greater power be introduced.*

Nowadays the 1.62 ball has been ousted by the American 1.68 and there are numerous formulations to choose from, which tends to add piquancy to the closing remark in the Chairman's speech at the above conference when he suggested that *a player should not be able to buy his shot in a shop.*

Soon after the 1914-18 war the officers of the many warships which used to visit Bournemouth in those days, were invited to play in friendly challenge matches. In one such it was said of a team from HMS Barham and HMS Malaya that *the course is a difficult one for those who have not played it before and therefore the sailor team accomplished a creditable performance by winning four of the thirteen matches.*

The first of the recorded Pro-Am matches was played on September 24th 1919 and resulted in an overwhelming victory for the professionals. In an effort to avoid such an unequal contest the format was radically altered in the following year. Secretary Morris' press release to the *Echo* is worth recording: *The Secretary.....gives notice of an unusual match between members and the professionals of the local clubs. In the past these have resulted in overwhelming defeats for the amateurs, so the teams will consist of twelve professionals and twenty-four amateurs. Each professional will antagonise (sic) a different pair of amateurs.* The announcement then listed the twelve professionals and the competing members and ended with *Admission to the course is free to golfers of both sexes. The clubhouse is a ten minute walk down St. Osmund's Road from the church, which is on the Lower Parkstone tram route.*

The result of the match was a win for the amateurs by 16 matches to 10. Major Grundy and Capt T Homer were all square after eighteen holes against E R Whitcombe, but lost to him on the 21st. In the afternoon they beat the Broadstone professional C Corlett at the 19th.

In March 1921 a special bus service was introduced from the Lansdowne in Bournemouth to the Ferndown Golf Club, which although completed in 1914, was not used for golf during the war years. It was scheduled to be formally opened on May 21st with an exhibition match between Duncan and Abe Mitchell, but this was cancelled and the course was not formally opened until October 1921 when Vardon and Ray played an exhibition match *in front of a large and appreciative crowd.*

Course maintenance

When the course opened its upkeep was in the hands of just one man, Charlie Hope, formerly of Fleet, who also acted as the steward in the clubhouse. The only other staff were Hugh Williamson the first professional and his assistant Padley.

It is difficult to imagine such a situation today; there were fifty-three acres of fairway and greens to maintain and all the work of mowing, rolling, fertilising, etc had to be done by hand. It should be remembered that in those days the course was a genuine links... sand and heather, so that the green fairways had to be *made,* literally. Many tons of soil were brought from local sources and this had to be carted and spread by hand throughout the course. The only transport was a horse and cart which was used to haul the mowers, rollers, and other course maintenance equipment, plus the water bowser, because there was no automatic system. However, the owners had a priceless asset, without which it is doubtful if the course could have survived the first year. They inherited a magnificent water supply which was probably unequalled by any other golf course. In addition to the two reservoirs and the Luscombe stream, the old water company installations included the substantial Victorian pumphouse adjacent to the fourth tee, beneath which had been constructed a huge underground reservoir capable of holding about three million gallons of water. When the course was constructed a water tower was erected on the viewpoint above what is now the eighteenth tee, and water was pumped to it to provide a sufficient head of pressure to feed a series of underground pipes to points around the course, to which hoses could be connected for watering the greens. A horse-drawn bowser was used for areas beyond the reach of the hoses. Some of the pipe outlets are still visible, but the water tower was dismantled in 1968 because it had been allowed to fall into a state of serious dilapidation. The course was watered through heavy rubber hoses which terminated in home-made sprinkler funnels, and the bowser had to be filled from the reservoirs by means of a hand-operated pump.

Parkstone should have resembled an oasis during the severe drought of 1911, but although there was no shortage of water, the greens were nearly lost simply due to the lack of manpower.

One of the two cottages alongside the pumphouse was demolished in 1986. These were originally built to house the waterworks employees and were not included in the sale when Lord Wimborne bought the land in 1910. The pumphouse and cottages were eventually included in exchange for the Ladies Walking Field on which now stands the Poole Arndale Centre. During the first phase of the golf club's history the cottages were rented out as summer retreats; the one now demolished was for some time used as such by the local Member of Parliament. In the days of the proprietary club the cottages were rented to two of the groundstaff, Charlie Major and Sid Baker, until they left the employ of the club during the Second World War. During the war the roofs were so badly damaged that the cottages were

Golf course maintenance c. 1921. The man with the bucket is George Gillett who was first employed in 1920 and became head groundsman in 1954. Raking the newly-sown seeds is his son Frank who eventually succeeded him and who remained with the club for 48 years.

deemed to be beyond economic repair and were sold in 1949 to a Mrs Russell-Brown for £1,500.

The fairway in front of the sixth green used to be a filter bed for the waterworks and a great deal of infilling was required to make up the required level. Observant members may be able to notice the different character of the ground in relation to the surrounding land.

Hope had to manage as best he could for the next eight years. In 1919 he was allowed to take on Frank Gillett a local lad who worked as a garden boy in Canford. Neither of them could have foreseen the effect of this move at the time; Frank was to devote the rest of his working life to the development and the upkeep of the course which he grew to love, to the extent that he refused a number of lucrative offers from other clubs, including it is claimed, one from Gleneagles.

Frank's father joined the staff in 1920 as Head Greenkeeper or Foreman Groundsman as he was known in those days. He had been an employee of the old water company and lived in the cottage nearest to the pumphouse, where young Frank was born. He stayed with the club until forced to retire due to ill-health in 1939, although he was retained in a consultancy capacity at a wage of fifteen shillings a week.

The groundstaff had no powered equipment during the whole of the period of private ownership; they mixed all their own ingredients for fertilisers etc and as the photograph on page 14 shows, applied it by hand, often working from five o'clock in the morning until eight o'clock at night during the Summer, all for less than two pounds a week. Frank's widow Laura recalls how she was often pressed into service as an unpaid assistant during the summer months, helping with the heavy hoses and whipping the greens.

The last job of the day was to bed down the horse which was stabled in a lean-to addition to one of the cottages. The old horse, which had served time in the Australian army, worked on the course until the arrival of the first tractor in 1928, he was then sold, together with all the accoutrements for £19.10.0.

End of an era

Lord Wimborne had been selling off some of his properties in Dorset and in 1927 was contemplating the sale of the golf course for building development. However he agreed to give members of the golf club the first refusal if they could come up with the necessary finance within a reasonable time.

Six prominent local businessmen formed a company to buy the land to preserve it as a golf course. Their fund-raising efforts however failed to reach the target of £20,000; they were successful in raising only £12,611 and were on the verge of admitting defeat when T W Simpson of Compton Acres came to the rescue with a low interest loan of £7,500. Simpson was desperately anxious to preserve the sylvan surroundings of his lovely house and the views across the harbour to the distant Purbeck hills. He succeeded in these aims during his lifetime and he undoubtedly played a great part in preserving the golf course, but the irony of the situation will not be lost on present-day members because it is Simpson's house which has been ravaged by the developers whilst the course and the lovely views remain to be enjoyed.... hopefully for ever.

This is the view Simpson sought to preserve when he loaned the balance of the purchase price to save the course from the builders in 1927.

The old 3rd green with newly-erected fencing to outline a building plot, which is now a well-established house and garden. The old 17th hole is in the background.

The old 12th (16th) with, in the background, a glimpse of the marshland and the waterworks cottages in their original condition.

General view of the course showing the recently constructed Lilliput Road and the old 3rd, 4th and 5th which were then played in an anti-clockwise direction.

2 *Uneasy partnership 1928 to 1960*

This view of the clubhouse is probably dated about 1950, but it still retains most of the original features.

2 *Uneasy partnership 1928 to 1960*

VERY LITTLE of a personal nature survives from this early period of the club's history, but fortunately one very early member survives who is able to recall events which occurred in the early 1920s. Reg Umney, whose father was a member and a dental surgeon in Bournemouth, remembers playing with his brother in the days when *the holes at the Lilliput end were played in an anti-clockwise direction and the fifth tee was in the corner by the crossroads where the village policeman lived.*

The Kitchin brothers, whose name is enshrined in a foursomes trophy were an integral part of the scene. Clad in long shorts the three of them played in all conditions *come hell or high water.*

Reg became articled to a firm of accountants in London in 1930, so he became a country member attracting subs of three pounds instead of six, which were reduced by a pound because he was one of three or more members of the same family in membership, then a further pound because he held twenty-five shares. On top of this he received twenty-five shillings dividend from the shares, and because articled clerks did not receive a salary for the first five years, he was entitled to a tax rebate on the dividend, so all-in-all he made a small profit out of his membership.

He bought a set of steel shafted clubs from Reg Whitcombe in 1932 for sixteen pounds and with them won the Long Handicap Cup and the Canford Cliffs Trophy. He recalls that Dunlop and Siver King golf balls were two shillings each, but that he had to be content with playing repaints which cost ninepence each. He also remembered that if one wanted to buy Reg a drink after the game, it had to be taken in the Steward's quarters.

The Branksome Tower Hotel was a popular rendezvous for the rich and the famous, and the Ambrose orchestra which played there regularly, were a familiar sight on the course... and they were notoriously heavy gamblers.

During the winter months, which appeared to be particularly severe, the water level in the smaller reservoir was lowered and ice skating became a popular diversion for the members, often by the light from the headlights of cars drawn up alongside what was then the second fairway.

The inaugural meeting of the shareholders in the new club was held on the ninth of January 1928. In the chair was Walter C J Shortt a Barrister living in Parkstone, who held one hundred shares. The other directors were Arthur W Moore, a Bournemouth architect, with one hundred shares; Arthur G Hamilton Brown, the major shareholder with one thousand shares; Wilfrid P Curtis, a solicitor from Parkstone with twenty shares; Arthur Biggs Chandler, a retired brewer from Bournemouth with fifty shares; Robert Kerr Fernie, a shipowner from Canford Cliffs with five hundred shares; and T H McMorland, a retired glass manufacturer from Branksome Park with one hundred shares; and fifty other shareholders.

The statutory report of the company listed the total number of allotted shares as 16,012, and the total amount of cash received as being £12,611.10.0. plus a loan of £7,500 at five percent interest from T W Simpson of Compton Acres.

The Parkstone Golf Club Ltd was formed at a meeting in the clubhouse on January 16th, 1928. Its members were *those who had applied for membership and had paid the annual subscription, and all those persons who have been invited by the company. Simultaneously a new club, to be called the Parkstone Ladies Golf Club would be formed as a branch of the Parkstone Golf Club with the same qualifying conditions.*

The initial membership of the new club was 234.

The new company started out with some very grandiose schemes; it was their intention to form a country club with indoor amusements and tennis and croquet lawns in addition to the established golf course. These dreams proved to be short lived however and the directors were forced to concentrate their efforts on maintaining the quality of the course, attracting visitors, and endeavouring to produce dividends for the shareholders.

They quickly discovered that the golf course had a large appetite for money and in those early years the golfing population was quite small. The Board therefore attempted to penetrate their target market by persuading a group of influential people to accept vice presidentships in the hope that by doing so they would introduce a high class clientele of fee-paying guests. They were successful in the first part of this campaign because the Bishop of London, Admiral Sir Nelson Ommaney, Major General W H M Lowe, Sir J H J W Jervis, and MPs Sir Henry Page-Croft and Hall Caine became members. T W Simpson, in appreciation of his low-interest loan which made up the balance of the purchase price of the club and course, was made the first president of the new club.

The Board moved quickly to mechanise the course maintenance work with the purchase of a Pattison tractor and triple roller, for an outlay of £188.15.6. which was slightly offset by the sale of the old horse and cart for £19.10.0. The objective was to restrict the number of groundstaff and to maximise the efficiency of the seven men now employed on the course.

There were no practice facilities for the members, so the directors asked for estimates to clear the ground which is now occupied by the first tee and the lower car park and the land which stretched out as far as what is now Alton Road East. The lowest tender was for £705 so the work was deferred *because of the great expense.* In fact the deferment became permanent because there is no evidence of any ground clearance and no further mention of practice facilities in the directors' minutes.

Charlie Hope the original groundsman left the club shortly before it changed hands, and the post of steward was awarded to G H Fisher who was at that time acting as barman. The arrangement was that his wife would act as a waitress, and their joint salary was fixed at three pounds a week. Fisher proved to be a very popular steward, but his term of office ended in 1944 when he was dismissed following an investigation into deficiencies in bar and catering accounts.

A slight mystery surrounds the identity of the caddiemaster in the cartoon on page 27. G F Prentice was the caddiemaster when the club changed hands and he remained in the post until just after the end of the war when he was replaced by C Woodman.

It must be assumed that the Harry in the cartoon must have been Prentice.

According to the directors' minute books for 1929, Prentice received no wages; he took a capitation fee from the professional on the caddie bookings, plus a commission on sales for the professional from the hut on the first tee, which amounted to about three pounds ten shillings a week in total. Caddies received one shilling and sixpence a round and an extra sixpence if they had to go out to meet their gentlemen at the tenth, which in those days was near to the present fifteenth tee. There was a path on to the course in those days and it was a very convenient starting point for members living in Canford Cliffs.

At the end of 1935 the commission arrangement with the professional came to an end when it was decided to stop the sale of goods from the caddiemaster's hut. This was a serious blow for Prentice, who applied to the Board for a weekly wage in lieu of this loss of money. The directors were indifferent to his plight and advised him that they were not responsible for any private arrangement he might have made with the professional, and that the terms of their agreement with him whereby they paid no salary but allowed him to retain a portion of the caddies' booking fee, were to stand. After further representations they

The 1st hole in its original layout. The main differences when compared with the view of the present hole (p. 106) are the lack of trees, no 18th tee and the massive bunkers on the left.

eventually relented and offered to pay him a wage of three pounds ten shillings a week, but he would have to forfeit his commission. This was not satisfactory to Prentice, but they eventually agreed on a compromise whereby the Board paid him a wage of twenty-five shillings and allowed him to keep his booking fee.

During all the discussions and deliberations which took place prior to the formation of the new club, the six promoters made overtures to Reg Whitcombe to leave Came Down to become Parkstone's new professional in place of Hugh Williamson who had been with the club since its formation in 1910. It would appear that Williamson was not making sufficient impact on the golfing scene to suit the new owners; in fact he was frequently referred to as the greenkeeper in local newspaper reports. Whitcombe was interviewed in the clubhouse in November and was appointed in January 1928.

Hugh Williamson was devastated by this turn of events. He was reputedly a shy and sensitive man, and he never fully recovered from the shock of losing his appointment. After a short spell in Switzerland and an abortive attempt to run an hotel in Derbyshire, he returned to Bournemouth where he ended his life in tragic circumstances.

The home green, constructed by the club's own groundstaff in 1934.

W C J Shortt, Barrister and Chairman of the company.

A G Hamilton-Brown, the largest shareholder

A B Chandler

R K Fernie

Four of the six directors of the company which bought the club in 1927.

MEL cartoon from the July 1937 issue of the Tatler magazine and reproduced by permission of the British Library.

Reggie, as he became known to members, remained with the club for the rest of his life and endeared himself to all who met him. He was promoted to professional at Came Down after his brother Ernest left in 1925. Prior to that he had been apprenticed to Ernest since leaving school at the age of fourteen. He enlisted in the army in 1914 but was invalided out with a heart complaint two years later and he worked as a greenkeeper/professional at Came Down until Ernest returned at the end of the war.

Eddie LeSuer, who became Reg's assistant at Parkstone in 1930, was a caddie at Came Down and was promoted from first-class caddie to assistant professional when Reg left. He learned his skills from Syd Realf the new professional who had a wide reputation as a clubmaker, a reputation which Eddie quickly acquired for himself. In the Spring of 1930 Eddie accepted the post of assistant to Reg and gave one month's notice at Came Down, but Syd Realf was so annoyed that he sacked him on the spot. This placed Eddie in a difficult position and he was forced to take a job as a stoker on one of the paddle steamers which operated between Weymouth and Bournemouth until he could take up his new job at Parkstone.

He stayed at Parkstone for twenty-two years and left to become the professional at Northbourne, where he stayed for just three years before moving to Broadstone. Sadly, Eddie died in 1985 but many of the present members remember him for his good advice, his playing prowess and his remarkable club-making skills.

In the October of his first year at Parkstone Reg was asked by the Board to invite his brother Ernest, Abe Mitchell and Ted Ray to play in a professionals' exhibition match, the latter for a fee of twelve guineas and twelve pounds respectively. Ernest had asked for a fee of ten pounds and the directors decided that if Reg could not persuade his brother to forego it, then they would agree to pay. Reg either failed to persuade his brother, or did not even try, because Ernest got his ten pounds and all four of them played before a large crowd of members and their guests.

Reg was appointed on a year's probation, and at the end of this period when he was confirmed in the job, the directors granted his wife Mabel the courtesy of the course *whilst R A remained as the professional.* In May of 1932 he received an additional fifty pounds a year to act as course supervisor. His

Eddie LeSuer, who joined the club as an assistant to Reg Whitcombe in 1928. He made the clubs Reg used to win the 1938 Open Championship.

retainer at this time was two hundred pounds a year, and it remained at this level until January 1945 when it was increased to three hundred.

During their first year of office the directors agreed to the formation of a general committee to run the golfing activities and to be responsible for the oversight of the condition of the course and the organisation of the golf competitions. The committee would not be allowed to incur any expenditure, but it could make recommendations to the Board through nominated directors who would be *ex officio* members of the committee.

In time the committee was allowed to appoint its own secretary, and the company secretary became known as the financial secretary, although much of his time was spent in discussions with his opposite number over the many contentious issues which arose between them. The members were jealously guarding their golfing interests and were suspicious of the Board's objectives, which it appeared to them, were concentrated on maintaining the right colour of ink on the balance sheet, to the detriment of the condition of the course.

Company secretaries came and went as regularly as the seasons, to such an extent that it is worth devoting a complete section to them, but the club secretary's task became more difficult as his committee's views became increasingly controversial. They wished to be consulted on every action of the Board which in any way impinged upon their golfing interests; they queried decisions; asked to be consulted whenever a new company secretary was appointed; and even asked for representation at Board meetings.

As can be imagined, the Board became angered by this constant intervention and at a very early stage offered to lease the club to the members. This offer was not taken up but the suggestion, either to sell or to lease, was made frequently, and it is an indication of the unhappy atmosphere which existed between the two bodies whose objectives seemed so divergent. Although when viewed from this historical vantage point, it appears that the majority of the members wanted the best of both worlds but were not prepared to accept any responsibility for ensuring the continuity of their good fortune. The course was by far the most popular in the area and attracted the majority of the *better class* of visitor; in fact, until the advent of the war the club was more often concerned with limiting the numbers than canvassing for new members.

The chief recurring complaint of the committee and one which had some foundation, was the reluctance of the Board to spend money on soil and top dressings. The course, because of its inherently sandy nature, dried out rapidly in the summer months, but the Board made only desultory purchases of soil and fertilisers, with the result that the staff was hard pressed to keep the course in good condition, especially in view of the heavy seasonal traffic it had to contend with. No specific or coordinated plan of course improvement emerged until Jack Stutt, with his specialised knowledge, joined the Board in 1952 and became head of the greens committee.

On every other count the Board's record of achievement in its first five years was very impressive: the course had been enlarged; the layout improved; mechanisation introduced to ease the burden of manual labour; and the staff had been increased. In addition electric lighting and heating had been installed in the clubhouse, together with a cold storage unit. In spite of this considerable expenditure the financial state of the company was healthy. The membership figures were climbing steadily in a controlled fashion, and the income from green fees was increasing: in 1928 there were 292 members and the course attracted over seven thousand green fees; in 1929 the figures were 458 and 8,639; and in 1931 the membership reached the declared saturation figure of five hundred.

On the subject of income, it is interesting to note that the Board allowed members of the clergy and bank employees to pay their entrance fee of five guineas in yearly instalments, and they allowed the Borough Engineer of Poole to spread his instalments over ten years.

There is no doubt however that the most important single achievement of the Board in these first few years was the decision to buy the marshy wasteland which flanked the western border of the course beyond the Lilliput Road. This was the culmination of a hard-fought crusade by Shortt the first Chairman of the Board. From the outset he pressed for the acquisition of the land from Lord Alington in the face of vociferous and unrelenting opposition from within his Board and from many other influential shareholders. The members, represented by the general committee, were unanimous in their opposition to the scheme. All contended that the land could not be drained sufficiently to make it suitable for use as a golf course. The majority were happy with the course as it stood and did not want any radical changes made to it. In addition many of the shareholders were opposed because of the delicate national financial situation which existed at the time.

It would appear from a study of the letters which survive that an important consideration in favour of the purchase of the land was to preserve the outlook over the harbour from the large and prestigious houses on the high points surrounding the course. The members and many of the directors who were not individually affected by the possibility of the development of the land as building land felt that the club was being held to ransom by the few who would be so affected. There were genuine fears of a national financial crisis in 1931, and one shareholder who opposed the scheme is quoted as claiming that the value of the one pound shares was as low as ten shillings, *so that it would be extremely difficult for the Board to raise the necessary finance.*

One member of the Board, and the major shareholder, went so far as to circularise the shareholders to oppose the scheme, and put forward an alternative layout which he claimed would have turned the course into a *Gleneagles of the South.* As a result of this, and wide support for the sentiments contained in the letter, Shortt, at a meeting of the Board in March 1931, tendered his resignation. This might have been a calculated last-ditch attempt to win over the support of the rest of the Board, but whatever his motives, the threat of his resignation certainly changed the outlook of the majority of his colleagues and they agreed to support his efforts and begin negotiations to buy the land.

As a result of the controversy with the members over this issue the Board withdrew its nominated directors from the general committee and cancelled the appointment of a special committee which had been formed to consider possible extensions and improvements to the course, and they again asked the members to take a lease of the clubhouse and course in order *to relieve the Directors of all responsibility and control which the members apparently desire to take on.* Finally the directors' letter to the committee ended with a thinly disguised threat that, in the event of the members not taking up the offer of a lease, they would *consult with the largest shareholders as to the future of the club and the Company's property.*

The letter appeared to have the desired effect in that it quelled the voluble opposition from the members, but they once again turned down the offer to buy the lease. However it did nothing to stop the genuinely held belief that the land would turn out to be a white elephant and that the club would as a result find itself in dire financial straits.

A meeting of the shareholders was held on the 24th of July 1931 to discuss the Board's proposal to buy the land, and in the following October a resolution to purchase, which was put to the shareholders at an extraordinary general meeting, was carried by twenty-eight votes to eighteen.

The share capital of the company was increased to £25,000 by the issue of three thousand additional shares, and a sufficient number of shareholders came forward with guarantees to cover the purchase price. The contract was finally signed in March 1932 whereby the club bought approximately sixty-three acres of Lord Alington's land for £5,000, which was one thousand pounds less than the original asking price.

In recognition of his efforts Shortt was appointed Managing Director of the company in the following May and he continued to serve in that capacity until 1947 when he became President of the club following the death of T W Simpson.

In the December of 1931, a year of considerable controversy within the club, Reg Whitcombe was made an honorary member of the club, but even this, which should have received unanimous approval, was tainted with ill-feeling. An informal discussion had taken place between the secretary of the general committee and the Chairman regarding the proposal and it was agreed that the Board would probably be in favour. Unfortunately the general committee then informed Reg before the Board was able to discuss it. They however decided not to risk the embarrassment of a rebuttal and allowed the appointment to stand, but this was yet another illustration of the depth of the rift which existed between the Board and the members' committee.

Draining the new land

In July of 1932 the Board commissioned James Braid to survey the land and to advise on its preparation and eventual incorporation into a new course layout. Braid prepared a plan which included a major re-design of the course and the addition of four new holes in the marshy new land. Based on this outline proposal, the Board sold off land in the Links Road area to pay for the cost of the development. At this time Links Road had not been made up and it belonged to the Company, as did Marlborough Road to the West and Alton Road to the North; they were not taken over by Poole Corporation until 1933.

Estimates for the digging of deep drainage ditches were invited from local companies, but they all proved to be too expensive, so it was decided to employ three local labourers to cut the drains under the direction of Charlie Major, one of the groundsmen. The work was supervised by a club member known as *C C*, a New Zealander who was the Dorset county captain that year, and who in the words of the Board secretary *had great experience of such work.* C C Roberts is another of the club characters depicted in the Mel cartoon on page 27, and he must have had the experience claimed by the Board because he became the course supervisor and remained so at a salary of one hundred pounds a year until 1946, when the Board decided to end the arrangement when the majority of the groundstaff returned to work after war service. As a reward for his services Roberts was made an honorary member of the club.

His position as course supervisor sometimes conflicted with the similar position held by Reg Whitcombe, and there is a complaint on record from one of the secretaries that the ground-

In the foreground is the 'new' 2nd, which dates the photograph at about 1935. The marshland in the background has been cleared and two new fairways can be seen.

staff were refusing to accept instructions from him, which is perhaps not surprising in view of the rather confused and confusing situation.

In the Spring of 1933 the land was ploughed to further increase the drying process, and on his next visit Braid declared himself satisfied with the preparatory work and recommended to the Board that Jack Stutt be engaged as the contractor to create the new layout. The Braid/Stutt combination enjoyed an enviable reputation as golf course designers, and during the golfing explosion which occurred in Britain in the 1930s they cooperated in the design or reconstruction of about eighty courses, including Dalmahoy and Rosemount, and in the reconstruction of Carnoustie to bring it up to the standard required for inclusion in the Open list.

The Board accepted the recommendation and work began in September 1933, with Braid acting as a consultant for which he received a fee of three guineas a visit.

Hamilton Stutt recalled in the notes he provided for the chapter on the evolution of the course that he remembered as a schoolboy travelling by car with Braid, who was a martyr to travel sickness. Braid would frequently have to stop the car to rush behind the nearest hedge. He was the professional at Walton Heath at the time and they were very reluctant to allow him time off for his course-designing projects.

The specification for the drains to be laid in the new ground survives in the directors' minute books, and Hamilton regards them as being of *Rolls Royce quality,* equal to the best installations of today. A price per yard was quoted for the provision of six inch pipes with top perforations, laid on 6 x 1 boards of Oak or Larch and covered with two feet of heather and one foot of clinker.

At his next meeting with the Board, Braid suggested moving the twelfth and fifteenth greens to alleviate the congestion, and the creation of the present second hole. These recommendations were also accepted and Jack Stutt's contract was broadened accordingly. Fortunately the secretary recorded the costings for this new work and they revealed that the cost of making the second hole was sixty-five pounds, which included removing the side of the hill to make the tee, putting in the bunkers, and turfing the green. At the same visit Braid had suggested the construction of a new eighteenth green, which at that time occupied the area on which stand the present Links Road bungalows, but the Board decided to leave this work to the groundstaff.

The total cost of the new construction work amounted to £2,565 which the Board was able to meet out of revenue, so avoiding the payment of tax. To complete the work, a new watering system was installed by Bacon & Curtis Ltd at a cost of £166, and a new pumping engine was bought to replace the worn-out unit which had been giving trouble for many years. The work was completed by the middle of 1934, but because the land took such a long time to dry out the new holes were not officially opened until the Autumn of 1937, although the Board bowed to pressure from the members and allowed play over two of the holes for about a year before the official opening.

The completion of the new course layout coincided with the beginning of a long wrangle with the Poole council over the vexed issue of the flooding of the lower part of the course with seawater, which was to continue for many years. To add to the problem, a much greater quantity of surface water was being directed into the Luscombe stream as a result of the building developments which were taking place around the course, and this would be further aggravated if a new town planning scheme prepared by the Borough Council were to come into effect.

An Artisan club

The idea for the formation of such a club was contained in a letter written to the Board of Directors by C R Maggs in November 1934. Maggs, who was a shareholder, suggested that the groundstaff should be given the opportunity to play on the course at specified times, and that they should be allowed to form a club which should include a small number of local work-people for the purpose of providing competitive golf, which he claimed would be an amenity and an incentive for the groundstaff.

The Board offered no objection and sent the letter to the general committee for them to consider, and if in agreement, to formulate a set of rules and regulations which would *safeguard the company's course and property*. It was discussed at a special meeting in the clubhouse attended by Maggs, Reg Whitcombe, Eddie LeSuer, George Gillett the head greenkeeper, and two members of the groundstaff Ernie Whitfield and Don Pollard.

The formation of the club was officially sanctioned by the Board in February 1935, when it was agreed that the subscription should be one pound, half of which should go to the company. Membership would be limited to twenty-five, who had to be living and working within three miles of the golf club. The groundstaff would be admitted for a subscription of ten shillings.

The golf club captain for that year was Herbert Adams who was well-known as a writer of detective stories; he was elected as the first president of the club. This established a precedent which was to remain in force for many years, whereby the captain of the *top club* as it was referred to by the early members, automatically became the president.

Don Pollard, one of the founder members, was one of a family of three Parkstone golfers, and his brother Albert, who had been on the groundstaff, left to become the first professional at Wareham when it opened in 1925, but he died at the early age of thirty-four.

The Artisans could claim a number of notable players in that first year; Don Pollard won the Bournemouth artisans competition and his success was later equalled by Ernie Whitfield who became the head greenkeeper in succession to George Gillett. The third member of the Pollard family also won the Bournemouth artisans competition in the following year. A Dawe, who worked as a roadsweeper in Poole and played off a handicap of two, won the Dorset amateur championship in 1935.

The members were allowed to hold their annual meetings in the clubhouse, but their regular committee meetings were held in the caddiemaster's hut until they obtained permission to build their own hut below the clubhouse in 1950.

The reservoirs were very popular with the members for boating and swimming in those days. The directors expressly forbade the Artisans to use them, but paradoxically caddies were allowed to bathe in the smaller lake, but only during the lunch period.

E West, the last of the original artisan members, died in 1983 and his ashes were scattered over the bank at the rear of the seventh green.

There were no artisan clubs in Dorset before the Parkstone club was formed, so when the boundaries were changed in 1974 the county trebled its number.

The club in jeopardy

1935 saw the beginning of a series of battles with the Poole council which were to continue up to and after the second world war. The first issue was the Council's intention to drain surface water from Compton Avenue into the reservoir; and then, following the passing of the 1934 Town and Country Planning Act, the Council announced its intention of declaring the golf course a public open space.

The efficient draining of the course was already a serious problem, due to the low-lying and marshy nature of the newly-acquired land, and the fact that the main drain through the Luscombe valley was over one hundred years old and incapable of coping with a new influx of water. In addition the Council's scheme would pollute the reservoirs.

In the face of the Council's determination to implement its drainage plan, the directors engaged the services of the retired Borough Engineer to study the scheme and its effect on the company's property, and to prepare a detailed technical objection. His report was formally presented to the Council, but it was rejected, so the Board decided to obtain an injunction and take the issue to Court.

On the very day of the hearing in London the Council relented and asked for an out-of-court settlement and the case was withdrawn. In the event the discussions between the Board and the Council dragged on for another four years, and the issue finally became a bargaining point in the Board's battle to salvage what they could from the very real possibility of the loss of their investment under the town planning scheme.

A settlement was signed in 1942 but was not implemented until after the war whereby the surface water was piped from the roads into a main underground drain which was constructed alongside the larger of the two reservoirs, and which ran beside the first and third fairways, across the sixth fairway and under the Lilliput Road into the large open ditch, which also collects the odd mis-hit golf ball from the eighth tee, then through the length of the ditch to the tide-operated discharge point in Poole harbour.

Members will be painfully aware that, following heavy rainfall or prolonged spells of wet weather, the water in the ditch backs up across the eleventh at just about the distance of a fluffed drive. This is due to the tidal nature of the drainage system; a flap valve at the harbour discharge point should open when the tide goes out to allow the system to drain, the incoming tide then closes the valve and the system fills up again.

As part of the settlement the Council undertook to maintain the open ditch and to ensure that the flap valve in the harbour remained in a serviceable condition, but such maintenance has been a bone of contention ever since.

The notification of the Council's intention to declare the golf course a public open space created understandable consternation among the Board of Directors, who became concerned either to wring the maximum possible compensation from the Council for the loss of their investment, or to contrive a compromise whereby the golf amenity could be retained in return for the sale of the land fronting the harbour which the Council wanted as part of a long-term development scheme for the town. The members for their part feared that they would lose their exclusive right to play on a course which they had helped to create, and of which they were understandably jealous.

It can be seen from the fold-out map that the property owned by the company in those days stretched beyond the present boundaries through to the Shore Road.

The letters reproduced on pages 42-44 give a clear indication of the fears of the Board regarding the possible loss of their investment, and of their endeavours to salvage as much as possible out of what appeared at the time to be a *fait accompli*.

A number of offers to buy the club were made at about this time, one from outside the club and at least two from within, but the terms offered were not satisfactory to the Board. As indicated in one of the letters, the Board themselves tried to sell the course to the Council on a lease-back arrangement, and as an added incentive the directors suggested that the twenty acres over and above the 150 acres of actual golf course could be sold by the Council, and that part of the proceeds could be paid back to the company by way of a reduction in the rent.

During the four years up to the outbreak of war the directors were in almost constant touch with the Council, trying to thrash out an acceptable plan whereby the Council could achieve its aims without too much loss to the company. However, it became clear that the Council was in a strong position, and as a final gesture the directors decided to lump together the question of

The small extension was made for Reg Whitcombe, but this photograph (c.1965) shows the clubhouse virtually as designed in 1911.

outright purchase with the vexed question of the surface water drainage of the roads adjacent to the course, which was a cause of great concern to the Council.

The directors proposed that the 150 acres of golf course should be designated a private open space, the other twenty acres not being used for golf to be sold, with the Council having an option on the Shore Road land. If the Council agreed the Board would allow the water drainage scheme to be constructed through the golf course.

The golf course and the other land belonging to the company was the largest tract of open space in the Borough, so it was understandable that the Council might display predatory tendencies. However, it would also be in their own interests to retain the golf course as an amenity but without the burden of upkeep, so a basis for compromise eventually emerged. The elements were the acquisition by the Council of a large tract of land fronting Shore Road which could be used for development under the town planning scheme; the preservation of a valuable amenity at no cost to the ratepayers, which as well as sustaining the high rateable value of the neighbouring area, also represented an amenity which attracted thousands of visitors, so enhancing the image of a town which had ambitions to achieve resort status; in addition the problem of the street water drainage would be solved. On the other hand, the directors of the golf club would secure the future of the course, they would be compensated for the loss of building rights and they would profit from the sale of land external to the actual golf course area.

This then was the situation which existed just prior to the outbreak of war when all such schemes were consigned to the town hall vaults, but it is roughly what happened when the scheme was taken out and dusted off after the war. The land to the West of a boundary formed by the eleventh green and a line along the fourteenth to the fifteenth tee was sold, and the golf course was declared a private open space. In 1959 the company received about £25,000 in compensation for the loss of building rights, and the drainage scheme was installed, although arguments and complaints about the consequent flooding of the course and the cleaning of the drainage ditch dragged on for many years.

Poole Town Planning Scheme
Parkstone Golf Course, 170 Acres

The Directors of the Parkstone Golf Club Company have intimated to the Ministry of Health their desire to be freed from this Planning Scheme. If however there is a serious inclination on the part of the Council to acquire sooner or later this area for the Poole people, possibly some form of gradual acquisition might be worked out to satisfy all concerned. The Council must however get rid of the idea that by using the machinery of Town Planning they can compel the Golfers to give up legitimate rights of property for nothing. A continuance of this contention only causes friction and leads to nothing.

Out of the 170 odd acres of land owned by the Golfers they are actually using about 150 acres as a Golf Course, which leaves roughly 20 acres available at once for sale for building purposes. This 20 acres is a compact block of land facing Poole Harbour and situated at the Harbour end of the Golf Course, with good frontage to Shore Road. This block controls the views and practically the amenities of the whole golfing area.

The Council might as a first step towards the acquisition of the whole area secure the immediate possession of this 20 acres adjoining the Harbour, and at the same time extinguish the building rights over the whole area of 170 acres. This would involve the payment of an agreed sum by the Council for (a) the purchase of the 20 acres with immediate possession and (b) the extinguishment of all building rights over the golfing area.

The second step which would be deferred for some years would be the ultimate acquisition by the Council of the then open space, some 150 acres, used as a Golf Course. The compensation for this would necessarily be a modest figure as building rights over the area (the most valuable part of freehold) would have been extinguished under step No 1.

July 1936

To
The Town Clerk
Municipal Offices
POOLE

Poole Town Planning Scheme
Parkstone Golf Course

Referring to the Conferences which have recently taken place between your Council Representatives and some of the Directors of the Golf Company, I am instructed by my Board to say they are prepared to lay the following proposals for the acquisition by your Council of the Golf Course lands before their Shareholders for confirmation after certain steps have been taken. The proposals are of course put forward without prejudice, and without admitting that the price suggested is even approaching the market value of the Company's Estate. All that my Directors have in view is an amicable suggestion for the transfer of the area to the Council, to be dedicated as a Public Open Space.

My Directors proposals are as follows:—

1 The sale to comprise the area of land believed to contain 170 acres more or less (but to be surveyed) together with the Club House and buildings (insured by my Company for £5725) and the Engine House and all other erections and buildings, together with the sites of two proposed roads respectively leading from Compton Avenue and Bingham Avenue to the Links; but excepting from the sale the pumping machinery and plant, and two pieces of outlying ground to be earmarked.

2 Except as hereafter stated the whole area referred to in clause 1 is to be forever maintained as a Public Open Space and the amenities as now enjoyed by all interested persons are to be preserved for all time.

3 The purchase price to be a minimum sum of £50,000.

4 On the completion of the sale the Council is to grant a Lease to the Company for 21 years of the lands Club House, Buildings, Reservoirs etc, now used for golfing purposes, estimated roughly at 150 acres, (but to be surveyed) at an annual rental of £1200. The Company to have the right to terminate the lease at any time on giving 2 years notice.

5 After the granting of the Lease it is estimated there will be more than 20 acres of land left in the Council's hands for immediate development as Public Open Space. Some outlying portions (to be agreed upon) of this 20 acres may however be sold by the Council, and should any sales be effected under this power, the agreed rent of £1200 is to be reduced from time to time by sums equal to 3% on the Capital moneys realized by such sales.

6 It is surmised by my Directors that the Council have in view some extensive draining of surface water through the Company's Estate. In the settlement of the terms of the Lease it will be necessary to insert clauses protecting the existing drainage of the Golf Course.

The early decision of your Building and Town Planning Committee, confirmed by the Finance Committee, is desired before any Meeting of the Shareholders (some 270 in number) can be called.

Yours truly
Lupton Robinson
Financial Secretary

August 1936

Chairman's memo re Town Planning and Luscombe valley drainage

So long as the building rights remain with the Golf Co. we are compelled to take every step possible to maintain their value as advised by Mr Deane (ex Boro Engineer engaged by Board to investigate the effects of new water loads). The cost of Mr Deane's proposals we are told may be put at anything under £30,000.

Should however the Council buy out the building rights for, say £25,000 under Town Planning, a different situation would arise, and the cost of Mr Deane's proposals possibly avoided. In such an event the Golf Company would be in a position to permit the entry of the abnormal supplies of water to their existing drains and ditches, but of course under conditions.

The existing system of drainage has been in use for more than 100 years, and it has been ample to carry away all natural supplies; but a large new influx may cause damage, and the Council would have to undertake to repair and maintain these drains in the future. .... The open watercourse .... would have to be regularly kept clean and open, and the cost of this would fall on the Council. Should it be found hereafter that these extra supplies were damaging the golf course by overflowing the banks of the stream, the Council would then have to provide some kind of pumping arrangement at the Shore Road. But this cost would not arise until the damage was shown.

The above is only a broad suggestion. There would of course be a number of details to be filled in. But what is worth consideration is the fact that the extinguishment of the Building Rights at an agreed figure of £25,000 may ease the position so far as the troublesome question of flooding is concerned. The Council would gain very considerably by having the cost difficulty as to flooding practically solved.

W C J Shortt
Chairman

May 1938

The secretarial scene

The administration of the new club was beset in the first few years by internecine struggles between the directors and tension between the Board and the members' committee. This uneasy atmosphere was probably a contributing factor, but whatever the reason, secretaries invariably departed the scene within twelve months of their appointment. There was one notable exception however, he was Lupton-Robinson who stood in after the departure of the first secretary and fluctuated between the posts of acting secretary, financial secretary, or joint secretary for nearly ten years.

C K Cotton was appointed soon after the proprietary club was formed, but his name appeared just once on the annual reports and he resigned in 1929 to take up a similar post elsewhere. He returned to the club and was eventually made an honorary member, but although the Chairman of the Board of Directors obviously wanted him to resume his old job, he was unable to persuade him, and Lupton-Robinson began the first of his locum tenencies.

A **Colonel Cochran** was appointed in January 1930 on a three month probationary period at a salary of £200 a year, but his period of office ended abruptly in the following October.

At a meeting of shareholders in March 1931, the Chairman, in reply to criticisms over his failure to appoint a new permanent secretary, admitted that he had been holding the job open for Cotton, but he said that he had not been able to persuade Cotton to return and that the Board had decided to appoint two secretaries, one to look after the company's affairs, and the other to look after the club members' interests.

Lupton-Robinson was confirmed as financial secretary, for which duty he received two pounds a week plus meals whilst he had to be at the clubhouse. In June 1931 the Board appointed **Commander Raymond** at a salary of £200, again for a trial period of three months. He was confirmed in his post after the probationary period, but he too resigned in the following April after less than one year in office. In May Lupton-Robinson, following a recommendation from the general committee, was officially appointed joint secretary of the club and company, but by the following October, the committee evidently regretted its decision and asked the Board to appoint another club secretary.

The directors' reaction to this prevarication is not known, but in December 1932 they appointed **E Hammond** to the post of club secretary. He became a comparative veteran in the post, because he stayed until the beginning of 1937, but in the latter part of his term of office he invoked the displeasure of the Chairman and many of the shareholders, principally because of his preference for the ambience of the clubhouse and neglect of his duties on the golf course. He was finally damned when the Chairman discovered that he had given up playing golf, so that his *resignation* soon afterwards came as no surprise.

The Board moved quickly and interviewed a number of applicants for the post, and within a month of Hammond's departure they appointed **Cope-Proctor,** who was then secretary at the Newquay golf club. He was appointed as joint secretary at a salary of £300, but this did not seem to affect the status of Lupton-Robinson who continued to attend the Board meetings. In June Cope-Proctor reverted to being club secretary with the loss of one hundred pounds in salary, and Lupton-Robinson again became the financial secretary.

Cope-Proctor was an experienced golf club secretary, but for some unknown reason the Board chose to issue him with a printed job description. Maybe they wished to avoid a repetition of their previous experiences, but the paper is reproduced on page 48 and makes interesting reading.

This situation remained unchanged up to the outbreak of war in 1939, when Lupton-Robinson died after about ten years service in and out of the post of secretary.

During the war there were only two changes; **A E Owen** did the work on a part-time basis after the departure of Cope-Proctor, until **R A Weaver** was appointed in 1944, also on a part-time basis. He was replaced in 1949 when **Major F A Latter** from the Haywards Heath golf club was appointed as the full-time secretary and for the first time in the club's history the members, through the general committee, were involved in the selection process.

E C Bond had acted as the club secretary (or match secretary as the post was then called), but these duties were gradually absorbed by Latter.

The name of **W B S Webb** appeared just once on the directors' annual reports, that was in 1955, but from 1956 until the company was formally wound up in 1961 **George Lawson** acted as the honorary company secretary, with **Douglas Bond** as club secretary.

With the formation of the members' club in 1961, Douglas Bond continued in the post of club secretary until his death in 1976, but for the last two years of his life he was a sick man, and **Group Captain David Bayne** was co-opted from the membership to assist him.

In 1976 the club appointed Claire Chauncy to assist with the office administration duties and together with David Bayne they produced an efficient filing and reference system, because Douglas Bond, although he could be relied upon to produce the required document when needed, always preferred to rely on his memory, his long experience in the job and his deep understanding of the membership... just so long as no one interfered with or *tidied up* his office. This was the practice adopted by so many golf club secretaries of his generation, but it was one which was likely to cause much anguish and frustration in the event of the absence of the incumbent.

After the sad departure of the much-loved Bond, Group Captain David Bayne acted as the temporary secretary until **Philip Bromley** from the Long Ashton club in Bristol was appointed in 1977. This was his first official appointment after completing a golf club secretary's course which he had taken with a view to providing for a happy retirement from his job with the Guinness company. Although popular with many members, Bromley resigned the position in October 1978. He was followed early in 1979 by **Bill Drury,** an ex captain of the Hayling Island Golf Club who had previously been a Senior Scientific Officer in the Diplomatic Service. Unfortunately he died in August 1982, but during his short period of office he proved to be an excellent secretary with a particular interest in efficient course maintenance.

Until the appointment of **David Thomas** in January 1983 the burden fell on the current captains and treasurers with Claire providing the thread of continuity which was so necessary for the smooth operation of the office, which, because it is usually the first point of contact, is a most important factor in creating a good impression upon the visitor. Esme Stuart-Smith and Eric Bond were always available with their long experience and sound knowledge of golf.

TABLE showing in a brief form the system adopted by the Directors for working the Company's affairs. The system has been gradually developed after five years' working experience.

The Company is responsible for dividends on a Capital sum of £22,000 which has been raised by issues of its shares. It is the owner of (inter alia) the following Assets:—(*a*) About 160 acres of freehold land, (*b*) A Golf Course, Club House, Cottages, and other buildings of all sorts, and (*c*) A Club with a Membership of about 450 (men and women), and it exercises its control and management of these Assets through its Board of Directors as shown below. The Board is more or less controlled by the terms of its Prospectus issued to the Public in 1927.

COMMERCIAL SIDE.

The Secretariat established in the Board Room and having its own Secretary doing the following work.

1.—All questions of finance connected with the Company and the Club which include (*a*) the collection of Revenue from the lands and cottages, the Club Members' and the Visitors' Green Fees, (*b*) the payment of Salaries and Wages to all officials and servants, (*c*) the sanctioning, checking and payment of all trade and other accounts, including the daily checking of the Steward's books and accounts.

2.—The keeping of all books of Account connected with the Finance referred to in No. 1, and having the same audited by the Company's Auditors.

3.—The keeping of the Company books connected with its Shareholders, and making Statutary returns under the Companies Acts, and the Company's Articles of Association.

4.—The preparation of the monthly Financial Statements.

5.—General Estate management as exercised by a land Company which includes (inter alia)—

(*a*) The protection of the Company's freeholds and other Assets.

(*b*) The upkeep and good management of the Golf Course.

(*c*) The care of the Water System and pipes, the Engine House and plant, and the Boundary Fences and Roads.

(*d*) All fire and other Insurances connected with the properties, and the Club, and its Members.

6.—The working out of a Scheme to provide funds to lay out the Alington lands by sales of building and other plots surplus to Golf Course requirements. The raising of funds for this purpose by Loans is not advised, or the policy of the Directors.

7.—The settlement of the difficult question of Town Planning under the Poole Town Planning Scheme as it affects the Company's lands, and the adjustment of the compensation payable to the Company.

8.—Generally carrying into effect the settled policy of the Directors to secure revenue from (*a*) the Course by efficiency of upkeep and necessary publicity, (*b*) improvements to the Club House such as the provision of a Common Lounge and bedrooms for the use of Members and Visitors.

GAMES SIDE.

The Club Secretary's office run by the Members and Games Secretary responsible for the following work and acting under the Committees appointed under the Golf Club Rules.

1.—The supervision of the Club House premises, the Steward, and the Club House servants.

2.—The supervision of the Professional and his staff, and Caddie Master and his staff.

3.—The supervision of the Golf Course, the Greenkeeper and Groundsmen, and everything necessary for the proper upkeep and maintenance of the Course.

4.—Attending to Members and their Games; Visitors and their Games. Attending to correspondence and Minute books, and records connected with the above work.

5.—Summoning and attending all Meetings of the Club Committees and recording their proceedings, and carrying into effect all decisions given after obtaining the sanction of the Directors when expenditure is to be incurred.

6.—Supervising the Club surroundings, including the parking places, and the parking of cars; the upkeep of the ornamental gardens and the roads to and at the Club House.

7.—Attending to the Advertising of the Course in Hotels and Boarding Houses, and arranging for the use of the Course by Organisations of all kinds.

8.—Generally furthering the work connected with the popularising of the Course and its attractions to Members and Visitors.

9.—Supervision of the Club House Library and all records connected with it.

The Co-ordinating officer between the above two Departments is the CHAIRMAN for the time being of the Directors in consultation with the Club Captain and the Sports Secretary.

Copy of the club secretary's job description issued to Cope-Proctor in 1937.

DAVID THOMAS was trained at Loughborough; represented the college at cricket, hockey, squash and tennis; and was selected for the English Universities at both cricket and hockey.

He played hockey for Hounslow, Middlesex, Wales, and Great Britain, gaining fifty international caps, including a tour of South Africa with the British team in 1951, and with Great Britain in the Olympic Games at Melbourne in 1956. In the middle fifties he also won a Middlesex doubles tennis title, and it was about this time that he started to play golf and joined Porters Park Golf Club. Towards the end of the sixties he left the teaching profession and was appointed as manager of the country's first dual-provision sports centres at Bingham, Notts, and shortly afterwards was appointed as the first Director of the National Sports Centre for Wales in Cardiff, where he continued to play golf at the Glamorgan Golf Club.

In 1974, he became the Chief Recreation and Amenities Officer for one of the Kent district councils, and joined the Sene Valley Golf Club where he eventually became the Club Chairman, and where his wife Helen served as the Lady Captain.

At the end of 1982 David retired from local government and took up his appointment in January 1983 as Parkstone's seventeenth secretary.

DOUGLAS BOND joined the club in 1931 and was secretary for twenty years, prior to which he was a member of the general committee and then on the Board of the proprietary club. He was appointed club secretary in 1956 and when the members bought the club in 1960 he agreed to continue as secretary *for a time,* which turned out to be sixteen years.

Prior to moving to Bournemouth he played his golf at Burnham and Berrow and retained his membership there after his move, returning in 1953 after an interval of thirty-nine years to win the club medal with a net 68.

Douglas was a cricket enthusiast and never tired of talking about the talents of Grace and Hammond. He played for the Wembley club and occasionally for his native Gloucester. Mrs Tula Bond was twice lady captain and played golf to county standard. Douglas himself had been a single-figure player.

He died in 1976 at the age of eighty-nine and was a much-loved member of the club. His tall upright figure moving briskly about the clubhouse belied his age and his long service.

Into the war and up to the 60s

In 1935 at the West of England Open Championship which in that year was held at Parkstone, Reg Whitcombe tied with brother Ernest 69 and 63. He won the replay with a 66, all three rounds being played on the same day. On the following day he won the *News of the World* tournament with a 63 and a 66, thus playing five consecutive rounds on the course for a total of 327, an average of just over 65 a round.

This truly remarkable feat puts into perspective the rather naive description of the course which appeared in a well-known golf journal at the time. The writer described the course in lyrical terms.... *heather to the right, heather to the left, makes a beautiful frame for the fairways, while dotted here and there are artistic sand bunkers cunningly planted to trap stray shots played by frail golfers.*

Even on a miniature scale the skill of the Whitcombe family was no less striking; the local paper carried a report of a unique golfing event which took place in Bournemouth in 1936, and it was the first occasion on which the Whitcombe family all played together. A nine hole course had been constructed in the half-acre *back garden* of a house in Leicester Road Branksome Park by Jackson, a prominent local architect, and supervised by Ernest Whitcombe, who was at the time the Professional at Meyrick Park. Sixty trees were cut down and four greens were laid, using specially imported turf. There were nine tees, each positioned so as to provide a different shot to the green. Three of the greens were used twice and the other three times. The length of the course was 326 yards, the holes measuring on average just over forty yards each, the longest being sixty yards and the shortest twenty yards. Each green was well bunkered and the flags were of a different colour and design to indicate the direction. Numerous hazards and rough were put in, including specially planted gorse.

The bogey for the course of eighteen holes was 54 and in the opening exhibition match Ernest scored 46, Charles (Crews Hill) 47, Ernie (Ernest's son and Assistant at Meyrick) 50, Reg scored 53.

The truly amazing skill of the Whitcombe family is further emphasized in a neat article which Henry Longhurst wrote for the *Tatler* just before the 1937 Open. The style of writing and the obvious feeling for the game is in marked contrast to the other quoted articles in this book.

I wonder if it is too late for Charles Whitcombe to win the Championship. Three times he has had his chance, only to find, as he engagingly confessed in a newspaper article, that his nerves were too much for him. Now he claims to have them under better control. As to the quality of his game in general, one can only say that he went around his native heath Crews Hill in 59 the other day. His figures were: 4-4-3-4-3-3-3-4-3 = 31; 3-4-3-3-3-3-3-3-3 = 28... ridiculous total, 59.

This extraordinary score was due of course to holing out in one on almost every green, but it brings one back instinctively to the old question of what is the ideal length of the golf ball. Sam King in the Sunday Referee commenting on Whitcombe's round said, this sort of thing means that the course is not being played as it was designed to be played. The tremendous distances obtained with the modern ball and clubs, coupled with the accuracy of a man like Whitcombe, simply leaves the difficult carries and hazards of bygone days standing. Home in two at any hole, and a drive and a kick at most of them, is the rule nowadays.

So far so good, but then he falls into the old trap that has ensnared so many people who have entered the discussion on the question of the ball. He suggests that the old-fashioned cross hazards should be restored, the bunkering at short holes tightened up, and the size of the greens reduced in order to stop Whitcombe going round in 59.

Oh dear, oh dear! Whenever will people realise that the object of us martyrs who cry out for a curtailment of the ball is not to stop anyone going round in 59, but to give him back the shots that the architect intended him to play. You can narrow the fairways, add to the bunkers, tighten up the greens, do what you like, but you still do not alter the fact that, if you keep the drive in play, a hole a quarter of a mile long is still a drive and a kick in the summer.

In the event of course, Charles Whitcombe did not win the Open.

The age-old controversy about the length of the ball was current as far back as 1912 as can be seen from the discussions between the R & A and the American golfing authorities which were briefly outlined in the first chapter of this book (page 11).

Returning to the Parkstone scene, Sir Leonard Lyle the sugar magnate was appointed to the Board in 1937, and he was later to figure in one of the many bids to buy the course which were made just before and in the years following the war.

One of the last of the original members of the proprietary club died in 1937, he was William John Augustus Price, a cousin of Lord Roberts of Mafeking fame. He had often expressed the hope that when it came his turn to die, it would be on the golf course. Well the Gods were kind to him because not only did he die on the course, but he was able to complete his round. The local paper reported that he died on the eighteenth tee *after hitting a sound drive to the green.* His ashes were scattered on the first tee.

Another of the more distinguished original members, and one of the first to be made an honorary member of the club, Admiral Sir Nelson Ommaney, died in the following year at the age of eighty-four. But 1938, in spite of the death of the venerable admiral and the looming war clouds, was the most notable year in Parkstone's history ... it was *Reggie's Year*... the year he won the Open after so nearly snatching it from Cotton's grasp in 1937.

Reg was feted by the club members and by civic dignitaries including the mayor and mayoress of Poole and the sheriff at a dinner at the clubhouse on his arrival back from the championship, and again a few days later at the formal reception at the Branksome Tower Hotel.

In a fulsome welcoming speech given by W D Simmonds the club captain, he referred to the occasion as *the greatest day Parkstone Golf Club ever had....the importance of it has passed the bounds which limit an ordinary sports event.* In reply Reg scotched rumours of his imminent departure from the club, he admitted receiving a number of attractive offers, but observed laconically, *there are better jobs, but no better place.*

The war brought a virtual cessation of competitive golf, not only at Parkstone, but especially in the South Coast golf clubs. Many courses were rendered unfit for play by the intervention of the War Department who ordered them to be ploughed up, either for food production, or to prevent the landing of enemy aircraft, and many were disfigured by the installation of anti-aircraft gun batteries, searchlight and barrage balloon sites.

Fortunately Parkstone was spared the worst of these indignities, and golf was able to be played throughout the war years, although on a scale restricted by opportunity and by the enforced attenuation of the playing area.

The groundstaff was reduced to two full-timers, Whitfield and Spinney, who were paid respectively four guineas and three pounds ten shillings. They were supervised by C C Roberts, of whom more appears in the section dealing with the draining of the Alington land.

The seventh, ninth and sixteenth greens were ringed with barbed wire to protect them from the hob-nailed boots of the soldiers manning the searchlights and anti-aircraft guns, and the tenth green was drastically reduced in size. The hole itself had to be turned into a par three, because there was a hutted encampment on the fairway and because of the searchlight battery near the green. Players had to walk back along the edge of the tenth fairway, cross the ditch in front of the eleventh and play from a small tee near the ditch. In addition, the ninth and tenth fairways were scheduled to be used as practice landing sites for cub aircraft, presumably as part of an *ab initio* training programme for potential RAF pilots, but it is doubtful if they were ever used as such.

The Board asked the War Office for an annual rent of £200 for the areas taken over by the military, but they had to accept £52 plus a claim for damages, which like all similar cases, would not be considered until after the war.

Even during this dismal period in the club's history, there was a great deal of internecine bickering over the operation of the club. The assets were valued at just under £25,000 and many shareholders were vociferously pressing for a revaluation with a view to selling-off the course and clubhouse. With the shares being quoted at only seven shillings and sixpence (about 37½p), the club was vulnerable to a take-over for potential property development. Fortunately there was sufficient support on the Board for weathering the storm and for maintaining the land as a golf course, but they were put under considerable pressure from within and from shareholders who were no longer members or who were living outside the area.

Mabel Whitcombe became the Stewardess of the club in the August of 1944, at a salary of £250, but in spite of her previous experience at the job in Came Down, she did not like it, and resigned in May 1945. Soon afterwards Mr and Mrs Sims were appointed at a salary of £220 plus a Christmas bonus of £30.

At about this time there were disagreements with the licensing authorities over the hours of opening of the club's bar, and especially on the proposal to open it on Sundays. The Board decide to create a Wine Committee composed of Dr Fitzpatrick and E C Bond, to be responsible for the general running of the bar and to control the purchase of supplies. The bar opening times were finally fixed at 11 to 2.30, and 4.30 to 9 o'clock on weekdays, and from 12 till 2 o'clock and 6 to 9 on Sundays, Christmas Day and Good Friday.

Catering had been reduced to the provision of simple snacks and sandwiches, so it is perhaps surprising that the Board should deem it necessary to appoint a full-time couple, and to employ their son on a part-time basis. However, they did increase the price of the war-time fare: a pot of tea plus one piece of cake went up from sixpence to ninepence (about four new pence); an extra piece of cake went up from twopence to three (old) pence; a paste sandwich from two to threepence; but the price of a meat sandwich (when available) remained at sixpence.

In February 1945 the Board received an offer from a syndicate comprising Sir Leonard Lyle, James Walker and G H Jordan to lease the course from the company for an annual rent of £3,000.

The Board, mindful of the substantial compensation they expected to receive from the loss of building rights under the town planning scheme, decided against leasing in case it prejudiced the outcome of the compensation negotiations. They did however, seriously consider an alternative proposition from the syndicate for the outright purchase of the club and its assets for £100,000. This too eventually came to nought, but a new offer, this time from H W S Palmer and favoured by a number of directors, for the purchase of shares at a price of 22/6d was bandied about for so long that Palmer lost patience and withdrew.

The company profits for 1945 were surprisingly good under the circumstances, but of course the situation owed much to the fact that no dividends had been paid for five years. The Board's decision to declare a ten percent dividend for that year was perhaps understandable, but it was taken in the face of an anticipated escalation of expenditure if the condition of the course was to be restored to anything like its former quality.

The Board had to raise more funds, so the annual subscriptions for new members were increased from five to eight guineas, and they asked the general committee to consider a similar increase for existing members. In the event it was decided to create two classes of membership; full members, who would pay eight guineas, and five-day members who would pay six guineas. This was modified soon afterwards when B L

Bisgood suggested that holders of twenty shares or more should receive a one guinea reduction, this was another unsuccessful attempt to persuade playing members to buy shares. They also decided to make efforts to increase the membership, but it is to their credit that they insisted on maintaining the high standards set before the war. New applicants were vetted very carefully, and the Board rejected quite a number of applicants who had been considered acceptable to the general committee. It is a pity that the Board's minute books do not contain any clues as to the criteria set, or the reasons for rejecting the unsuccessful candidates.

In view of these moves to bolster the club's finances, the increase in Reg Whitcombe's retainer from £200 to £300 could perhaps be regarded as generous.

The assets of the company were shown in the balance sheet as being worth just under twenty-five thousand pounds, which was

This fine example of Victorian industrial architecture once housed the pumping machinery for the waterworks. It now contains the pump and automatic controls for the course watering system, and is used to garage the course maintenance equipment.

obviously much less than the true value of the club, but although they commissioned a local estate agent to re-assess the value, based upon the use of the land as a building site, they were persuaded by C G Lester, acting as honorary solicitor to the Board, to defer any action pending the outcome of negotiations with the Poole council over compensation under the Town and Country Planning Act.

In April 1945 John Clark offered to sell to the club his house above the fifteenth green. The prospect of revising the layout of the course to permit two convenient starting points and of building a clubhouse in the centre, was very attractive and it excited the interest of a great number of members. However, the ever-present shadow of the Town Planning Act and the compensation attaching to it, again coloured the Board's deliberations, and they eventually decided that it would not be sensible to proceed. The opportunity to greatly improve the layout and the facilities was therefore lost, and the block of flats known as Forsyte Shades now dominates the skyline above the fifteenth.

By the latter part of 1945 the demand for catering under the stewardship of the Sims family had increased to the point where she was asked to provide hot and cold luncheons, at the respective charges of 3/6 and 2/6 (17½ and 12½ new pence). As an

Ken Longmore, Reg Whitcombe, Jeanne Bisgood and Leonard Crawley in an exhibition match to celebrate the opening of the revised 12th hole in 1955. Reg was unwell, but his partner Ken Longmore was in fine form, going out in 33 and scoring a birdie at the new hole. Jeanne played from the men's tees and received seven shots, but she and Crawley were beaten 3 and 2.

incentive the Board offered to pay a commission of 5% on the first £100 per month of catering takings, and 2½ % on amounts above £100.

From November 1945 the green fees were increased to 5/- on weekdays and to 7/6 a round, or ten shillings for the day at weekends. On bank holidays Christmas and Easter the fees were increased to ten shillings a day, and the concession of reduced fees for visitors with members was cancelled.

At the same meeting, the Board decided to waive the subscriptions of Miss Drinkwater who had been the secretary of the ladies club for ten years. She was later made an honorary member of the club.

An interesting sidelight on the events of the day is provided by a decision of the Board to waive the outstanding subscription of two guineas for Mr S P Hey who had lost his clubs. Members had been complaining about trespassers on the course, especially at weekends, and after much pressure from the general committee the Board agreed to pay ten shillings per attendance for a ranger to patrol the course on Sundays during the summer months.

By mid 1946 the work associated with the club aspects of the secretary's work had increased to the point where the Board agreed to the appointment of E C Bond to act as games sub-secretary at a wage of one pound a week. He was to work with the part-time secretary R A Weaver *to be responsible for organising competitions, prizes, sweepstakes, keeping games records, and looking after the handicaps.* He would also *assist members and visitors to find games at the weekends.*

T W Simpson of Compton Acres whose financial assistance made possible the purchase of the club from Lord Wimborne, died in 1947. A few months later W C J Shortt resigned from the position of Chairman of the Board due to ill-health, and C G Lester was appointed in his place. Shortt was made President in 1948 but lived for only two years after his retirement. During this time he continued to attend meetings and to act in an advisory capacity and he and his wife were made honorary members in recognition of the long and valuable service he had given to the proprietary club. He was undoubtedly the major force behind the campaign to raise the money to buy the course in 1927; the prime mover in the acquisition of the Alington land; and in pressing for a complete revision of the course in the

1930s. It is also obvious from the records which remain, that he was the *strong man* of the Board and was chiefly responsible for fending off the many attempts to sell the course to outside bodies.

In December 1948 Bertram Bisgood, who for some time had acted as the company's legal adviser, was elected President of the club in succession to Simpson, and he and his wife were made honorary life members.

The condition of the course continued to cause concern; the desultory purchases of fertilisers and soil were having little effect, and it would appear that the groundstaff lacked the necessary guidance to deal with the problems caused by five years of virtual neglect, plus the damage created by the military occupation. In addition, there was no-one on the Board sufficiently qualified to prepare a coordinated plan of revitalisation. Much was said in the reports about the need to bring the course up to its pre-war standard, but little was done by way of expenditure or professional advice until the latter part of 1947 when the Board of Greenkeeping Research was asked to send a specialist to examine the course and to recommend a plan of refurbishment.

The report, which recommended, among other things, that a great deal of the rough should be cut back, and that intensive treatment of the moss problem on the greens should be undertaken, was debated by the Board at a special meeting and they decided after considerable pressure from the general committee to accept the report and its recommendations in its entirety. Reg Whitcombe was directed to supervise the work; two men were employed to cut back the rough and £100 was to be spent on materials plus another £300 on equipment. In addition to the work on the course it was decided to take up the mown heather which formed the putting green at the clubhouse and to replace it with grass grown from seed. Heather putting surfaces were not uncommon in the early days of golf course construction, no doubt emanating from the old Scottish practice, but they would not stand up to heavy wear and constant mowing.

In June 1948 a long discussion took place at the Board meeting on the subject of the management of the club, and they decided to act with the general committee on a joint basis to consider vesting the management of the course and the clubhouse in the members at a rental which would be acceptable to the shareholders. It would appear that no satisfactory scheme could be agreed upon, in spite of the evident need to secure a more amicable form of management, and also in spite of strong encouragement from Shortt the retired Chairman, W D Simmonds, and B L Bisgood. Discussion went on for nearly twelve months, but in the event nothing of significance evolved from the meetings, and the barely concealed disharmony between the Board and the general committee continued...and was to do so for another decade.

All that came out of the discussions was a decision to re-decorate the clubhouse and to make some long-overdue alterations to the dining room; the provision of hot water in the kitchen; the installation of a shower-bath in the men's locker room; and a general refurbishment of the ladies rooms. (In a later meeting, the Board decided against the shower-bath on the grounds that it would not be used). The opening hours at the clubhouse were also amended, lopping off a quarter of an hour in the morning and extending the closing time during the summer months to 9.30 instead of 9 o'clock. In addition, the Directors consented to the construction of a new 12th green to the west of the existing one, and to make a new tee for the 13th. These recommendations had previously been turned down by the Board because they felt that they should have been included in the major re-construction of the course, based on Braid's revised layout in the 1930s. When this work was completed, a new tee for the second hole was constructed, and the old, elevated tee abandoned. The groundstaff had often criticised the layout of this hole because shots from the elevated tee created deep pitch marks in the surface of the green.

As a further concession, the Board agreed to employ a full-time secretary. Weaver had been acting as a part-time secretary since 1943, and E C Bond was acting as match secretary. There had been no previous intimation that Weaver wanted to give up, or that the Board was dissatisfied with his work, so it must be assumed that his replacement was a genuine concession to pressure from the general committee.

Major Latter from Haywards Heath was chosen from one hundred and thirty applicants. He took over in February 1950 and E C Bond relinquished his part-time post after a couple of months. As mentioned in the section dealing with the secretarial changes, the Major experienced some difficulty in persuading the groundstaff to accept his authority for work on the course; one of them resigned shortly after the appointment and another was sacked, but after these early hiccups he settled down and proved to be a good choice.

At about this time the Sims family, after complaints from the members of poor service and intervention by the wine and house committee, left the stewardship of the clubhouse and were replaced by a Mr and Mrs Corbishley, but they too were soon being complained about and were asked to leave in 1951. They were followed by the McFarlanes; she had previously served as a waitress in the club for about eighteen months and he had been in the Navy, *but had experience of bar work.* They lasted no longer than their predecessors, and following complaints of poor service which was reflected in a severe drop in the takings, they too were asked to leave and they were replaced by Mr and Mrs Hughes. The complaints about poor service and the high turnover of staff were not entirely the fault of the stewards because the accommodation and the facilities provided for the staff were to say the least basic, and they were not greatly improved until shortly before the transfer of ownership to the members.

The general committee persuaded the Board to allow Reg Whitcombe to run a golf school for the young people of the district during the school holidays. The idea was for Reg to teach them the rudiments of the game and course etiquete, and when he was satisfied they would be allowed to play at times when the course was not busy for a fee of 2/6d. There is a photograph in the club scrapbook which shows Reg posing with a group of about twenty youngsters, but there is no record of how successful the scheme was, or how long it lasted, but the lack of practice facilities would have interfered greatly with the development of such a scheme, however worthwhile.

The final attempt to persuade the members to take a lease on the club and to run it for themselves was made in 1950, but it too failed, and for the same reasons as in previous years....a lack of funds and a strange reluctance on the part of the members to recognise the danger they faced from a possible takeover. Only twenty-one percent of the members were shareholders, and only eighteen percent of the total number of issued shares were held by the members of the club. The rest were in the hands of trustees or the families and friends of the original holders, many of whom were not golfers and not resident in the area, so that they had no interest in the amenity aspect of the club. In addition, the dividends they had received for the greater part of the life of the company had been niggardly...rarely above five percent; so that there was a genuine risk of them grouping together to cash in on what had become an extremely valuable asset.

Towards the end of 1951 the Board had become very concerned about the financial position of the club. The membership had fallen to 203 men and 131 ladies, with a consequent loss of subscriptions and entrance fees, although the income from green fees, at nearly two thousand pounds, showed a slight increase over the previous year. There was a loss of about one hundred pounds on the revenue account, and this was explained by the necessary repairs and redecoration of the clubhouse, but the loss would have been much greater if it had not been masked by quite sizeable transfers from the members' account to the company account. No dividend was declared for that year and in an attempt to improve the situation, subscriptions for new members were increased to ten guineas for men and eight guineas for ladies, and a special joint subscription was introduced for husbands and wives of ten guineas plus the appropriate entrance fees.

By the end of 1952 these measures, plus a marked increase in the takings from the bar and dining room, combined to put the club back on its feet, and it was decided not to increase the subscriptions for existing members.

Two very popular events which took place on the course at this time and which lasted for nearly twenty-five years was the Branksome Towers Spring and Autumn meetings. These attracted many low handicap players from clubs in the London area, in addition to the best of the Parkstone club members.

Alas the hotel is no more, but in its day it was the favoured haunt of Royalty, titled families and the most famous personalities of the day. For example, the Duke of Connaught stayed at the hotel regularly for very many years.

The nameplate from its door was presented to the club by Dr Donald Holmes and is now set in the concrete base of *Tommy's Bar* above the twelfth green as a permanent reminder of the close links which existed between the club and hotel for so many years.

The event began in 1929 when golfers visiting the hotel were

Miss Mary Llewellyn, the first Lady Mayor of Poole was the guest of honour at the 1951 Branksome Tower meeting dinner. Roy Jenkins and John Clark won the Salvers, and with them are club secretary Major Latter, a portly Reg Whitcombe, and Vernon Haydon.

invited by T H Vernon Haydon, the director and manager, to take part in a seventy-two hole competition on the course. They originally played a foursome competition for a pair of silver salvers, but as the event grew in popularity so did the number of trophies until at its height there were fourteen prizes on offer.

The invited golfers met at the hotel on Friday evening and after dinner, amid the cigar smoke and liquers, an auction for the players was held, which often ran into a four figure total, so some of the golfers were playing for high stakes.

The main event was for the salvers, but in time there was a Founders' Trophy, decided over the first two rounds; a cup for the best scratch score; a handicap trophy; an eclectic cup; and various other prizes including Henry Cotton wallets for the best scores on seven sealed holes.

The meetings seemed to attract golfers especially from the Addington and Sunningdale courses, and one newspaper feature in 1950 listed four plus-one, three scratch, and several one and two handicap players among the forty-two competitors.

The Golf Illustrated journal organised the 1937 Autumn meeting and reported that a scratch golfer from Beaconsfield won the Challenge Cup over thirty-six holes, with scores of 73 and 75. This was a remarkable achievement under the circumstances, because it was the first competition to be held over the revised course, which had been stretched to an SSS of 74 by the addition of the new holes in the recently acquired marshland, and five and a half inches of rain had fallen during the previous four days, so that the course must have resembled a bog.

The runner-up in the thirty-six hole handicap was P Stuart-Smith who was then a four handicap player at Northbourne (now Knighton Heath), he returned nett scores of 77 and 76. Stuart joined Parkstone in 1939 and still plays steady golf in spite of the painful handicap of an artificial hip joint.

Henry Cotton the Open Champion presented the prizes and attended the last evening's celebrations whenever he could.

In later years John Clark and Roy Jenkins were the most consistent Parkstone winners, with Ernest Millward the English Amateur Champion, Joe Austreng, and Vernon Haydon, who figures in a number of long driving records, making quite an impact. Roy ruefully recalls choosing one of the meetings to score a hole-in-one at the eighteenth, *with whisky at only two shillings a nip, the round still cost me fifteen pounds.*

In 1945 John Clark bought the house known as Forsyte Shades above the fifteenth green for £15,000 and offered it to the club for the same figure, but for the reasons set out earlier, the offer was not taken up.

It would appear that the original idea to site the clubhouse above the fifteenth belonged to Reg Whitcombe. During a regular fourball game with John Clark, Roy Jenkins and Leslie Reynolds he pointed to the house and exclaimed *now that's where the clubhouse should be, we could then have two nine-hole loops.* John Clark took him at his word and bought the house as soon as it became available. He lived in it for a few years after the club rejected his offer, during which time it was the scene of many noisy parties, but he eventually sold the house and bought the Poole Harbour Yacht Club.

During this time the twelfth hole was a slight right-handed dogleg playing to a green under the hill at Compton Acres. A bank ran diagonally across the angle and contained a Rowan tree which often interfered with a good tee shot or the shot to the green. Reg is known to have complained about the tree on many occasions, but John Clark, who had a reputation as a surreptitious tree-feller, arranged to have it cut down during the night before the 1948 Branksome Towers meeting.

It is to be hoped that a similar fate does not befall the *infamous bush* which often wreaks havoc with a drive from the medal tee on the eleventh.

Charles Lester resigned as Chairman of the Board in May 1951, due to ill health, and W D Simmonds was appointed in his place, but Lester was able to resume his position after about twelve months and he remained as Chairman for a further two years until Jack Stutt was elected to the office.

Jack Stutt joined the club in 1947 after moving down from Scotland and he soon became active in pressing for a coordinated plan to improve the condition of the course. Even before he was elected to the Board in 1952 he provided, at his own expense, machinery for removing many of the small hillocks which interfered with the use of course maintenance machinery, and he also loaned the club a tractor-mounted scoop to remove the concrete foundation slabs which remained from the war-time military occupation of parts of the course. He and his son Hamilton pursued a policy of garnering shares whenever they became available, with the avowed intention of doing what they could to safeguard the club against a take-over. They became the major shareholders in the company, and this must have helped to overcome the opposition to his ideas for long-term course improvements when he was appointed to the Board. Inevitably the balance sheets began to show a marked increase in expenditure on the course, and for the first time in the history of the club a coordinated plan of maintenance and improvement was introduced which resulted in the elimination of many of the minor imperfections which interfered with the use of machinery; the easing of hills and steep climbs; and perhaps most important of all, the sustained strict control of the groundstaff in the programme of reseeding and top dressing of the greens and fairways.

Despite his insistence on increasing expenditure on the course (or perhaps because of it), Jack Stutt was elected Chairman of the Board in 1955 and, at the first shareholders' meeting after his appointment, Bertram Bisgood raised the question of a members' take-over. Jack expressed his wholehearted support for the move, but said that the initiative would have to come from the members. So began the move toward the change which so many people had wanted but which had been frustrated for so long by the twin evils of lack of money and the will to overcome the apathy of many of the members.

The year 1956 began on a black note with the death of Reg Whitcombe. At the memorial service in St. Luke's church in Sandecotes Road the church overflowed with members who genuinely felt the loss of a man who had been more of a friend than a club professional. Many examples of his philosophical approach to the game and to members' problems have been recounted, but they can all be summed up by the simple fact that his estate, after more than thirty years as a professional and winner of the greatest prize in golf, amounted to no more than a few hundred pounds....mute testimony to his frank and friendly way of life.

The club arranged a testimonial match in 1958 and raised over one thousand pounds for his widow Mabel.

From the large number of applicants for the vacant post the directors chose the Alliss brothers from the nearby Ferndown club; Peter to represent Parkstone on the tournament circuit and Alec to attend to the members' needs from the professional's shop.

As readers will be aware, Peter went on to achieve many notable successes at home and abroad before succeeding the illustrious Henry Longhurst as the BBC's number one golf commentator. These successes undoubtedly contributed to the increased popularity of Parkstone, from golfers keen to play *his* course, to well-known professionals and celebrities whom he encouraged to attend tournament and charity exhibition matches on the course. Typical of these was the *SPARKS* society, a group of sportsmen pledged to aid research into crippling ailments. In the 1963 visit eight pairs of golf professionals and well-known sports personalities were watched by a crowd of 3,000 and raised £400 for the charity.

A climate favourable to a membership buy-out was finally created by the payment to the Board in 1959 of the compensation for the loss of building rights under the Town and Country Planning Scheme, which in effect devalued the course by about £25,000. By this time the majority of the shares in the company were held by the Stutt family and by George Lawson, both of whom were keen supporters of member ownership. It was their generosity which made the change possible, aided by the unanimous support of the remainder of the Board, which consisted of John Brooks the Vice Chairman, George Vivian, Douglas Bond, George Newton, Greville Humphris and W D Simmonds.

Prior to the publication of the official proposition much private discussion took place between Stutt and Lawson and Ken Robshaw and Jim Buchanan, who was the Vice Captain of the club and a practising solicitor. He attended to all the legal details, organised the meetings between the Board and the members' representatives, and negotiated the financial arrangements.

In a letter to the members, which is reproduced on page 70 Geoffrey Iles the club captain explained that member ownership was at last a practical proposition, provided that a figure acceptable to the shareholders and the members could be agreed upon.

There is no doubt that, based upon the price of £20,000 paid to Lord Wimborne in 1927, the figure of £12,000 suggested by the Board was to say the least, extremely generous, and it is no secret that it aroused serious objections from many shareholders, of whom approximately two thirds were not members of the club.

A more practical figure, based upon the greatly improved assets and the potential earning capacity, would have been somewhere in the region of £50,000. It therefore says a great deal for the determination and the persuasive powers of the main promoters that they were able to overcome the objections and obtain the acceptance of the proposition by the required majority of the shareholders.

In spite of this nominal figure the club was unable to raise the money and the buy-out was eventually made possible only by a loan of approximately half the amount from Hamilton Stutt.

Twenty-two shareholders attended the extraordinary general meeting in the clubhouse on the fifteenth of December 1960 and, including the votes of the seven directors, twenty-six voted in favour of the resolution, with the three lady shareholders abstaining. Out of the proxy votes received, forty-two were in favour and three against. One hundred and forty-five failed to respond to the notice.

For their part the club members met in the Sandbanks Hotel on November the seventh, under the chairmanship of Bertram Bisgood. The proposal and the effects of member ownership were discussed at great length and the support, although by no means unanimous, was sufficient to carry the day. So, after half a century of private ownership, with the club membership standing at about five hundred, and with the course radically changed from Willie Park's original layout, Parkstone set the example for its sister club Broadstone, whose history had run a similar course, and achieved member ownership.

At the winding-up meeting of the company in the clubhouse on Wednesday the third of March 1965, with the members' mortgage repaid and all other assets disbursed, John Brooks the Vice Chairman made the following speech, which makes a fitting end to this chapter and to an eventful era in the history of the club.

I am pleased to second the proposition (to voluntary wind-up the company). This is just a formal meeting with one object clearly defined and I consider the Chairman has dealt adequately with the position.

Before the proposition is put to the meeting there is one other matter I would like to refer to.

After the proposition is carried the Liquidator takes over and this may be the last opportunity of expressing and recording what I consider should be said, and for the sake of accuracy of any record that may be made I have decided to write and read my remarks.

Being members of the club you will have received the general report to the members and will have read the first sentence in the final paragraph. It reads as follows:- "Finally I would like to remind members of the valuable service rendered by our President and past Captains, whose forward thinking enabled the members to acquire the club and course".

I make no criticism of what is stated but I wish to add to it. I can reveal that several years ago the Directors of the company were unanimously anxious to find a way of substituting a members' club in place of the limited company. The Chairman at that time was Mr Lester and the Vice Chairman Mr Johnson—respectively a solicitor and a Chartered Accountant—and being the two Directors best qualified to deal with such a matter they undertook to try to devise a way by which the transfer could be brought about. They ultimately reported to the Board that they had been unable to solve the difficult problem so the matter was left in abeyance, but not abandoned. As new Directors were appointed the desire to bring about a members' club grew stronger and over the years immediately before the solution was found—by the present Board of Directors—the search for a formula was always uppermost in the thoughts and even the plans of the Board.

I feel that this should be recorded in fairness to past and present Directors and to shareholders, for without the generous cooperation and forward thinking of both, a members' club would not have been possible.

I now have pleasure in Seconding the Resolution.

Dear Member,

Parkstone Golf Club

This is the further letter promised in my circular letter addressed to all members on 11th October 1960. The intention is to set out the reasons why your Committee consider it would be desirable for the members to acquire the course from the Parkstone Golf Club Limited, to report to you the result of negotiations which have already taken place, and to recommend to you a method by which such acquisition may be carried into effect.

1 I think that in the first place an explanation of the present arrangement is desirable. The course, clubhouse and equipment are owned by a public company known as the Parkstone Golf Club Limited. This is a company formed by certain members of the Club in 1927 for the purpose of acquiring the course from Lord Wimborne.

2 The articles of Association originally gave Members of the Company, and in certain circumstances Members of the Club, rights of pre-emption over the shares, but these rights were removed by an alteration in the Articles in 1947. The shares are therefore freely transferable, subject only to a power for the Directors to refuse to register transfers in certain circumstances.

3 Under the present arrangements all financial matters are under the control of the Board of Directors of the Company, who fix entrance fees, subscriptions and green fees and deal with all matters involving expenditure. The most the elected Committee of the Club can do in such matters is make recommendations to the Board. In addition the Board must pass all applications for membership, and have the right to nominate (8) members on the General Committee.

4 There has long been a feeling among members of the Club that this arrangement is not satisfactory, and this view is shared by the elected members of your Committee, whom I will hereafter refer to as "the committee". While these views have been held for some time past, it has been impracticable to take any action so long as the value of the course included development value, but the company has now received a substantial sum of money for their development rights. The reasons for the Committee's opinion are as follows:-

(a) It is not satisfactory for a private members club to be owned and administered by a public Company. It does not require much imagination to envisage circumstances in which the interests of the Club and the shareholders could be at variance.

(b) In the event of the management of the Company becoming inefficient there is no method at all whereby the members can bring about a change. The Directors are elected by the shareholders of the Company, who may or may not be members of the Club. I should make it clear that we are not seeking to criticize the present Board, whose administration of the Club is, I think, excellent, nor do I wish to suggest that there has been any lack of goodwill between the Board and the Committee. It is obvious however that this happy state of affairs could very easily come to an end, as times change and new personalities come on the scene.

(c) Under the present arrangements the shares of the Company might easily come into the hands of persons whose objects and intentions were in direct conflict with the interests of the Members of the Club.

5 These are all long term considerations, having regard to the present state of the Club, but they are nevertheless important. The Committee entered into preliminary negotiations with the Board to see if the Course could be acquired from the Company and if so upon what terms. After a number of friendly meetings it was agreed by the Committee and the Board that recommendations on the following lines should be made both to the Members of the Club and to the shareholders of the Company:—

(a) That the Company should sell and the Club buy the Course, Clubhouse, Goodwill and Equipment at the price of £12,000. Certain land between the 11th fairway and Shore Road would be excluded, as would certain building sites, and the site of a proposed electricity sub-station between the 8th fairway and the road. Fertiliser Stocks would be included.

(b) The consumable stores in the Clubhouse would be taken over at cost.

(c) The Company would leave the whole of the purchase money on loan, repayable by yearly payments of not less than £600, with interest at 6% per annum on the balance for the time being outstanding.

(d) That the transaction be completed on the 1st January 1961, or as soon as possible thereafter.

6 This then is the proposal which will be placed before you on the 7th November. Now I will deal with the manner in which it may be brought about. The whole object is that the ownership, administration, and finance of the Club shall be in the hands of the members. It is however necessary to have a body which can own the property, and give adequate security to the present Company for the money borrowed.

It is suggested therefore that the Course should be acquired by a Company Limited by guarantee formed by the Members of the Club. A Company Limited by guarantee is a Company which has no share capital, but each member of which guarantees a certain sum (say £10) in the event of the Company being wound up during his membership of the Company, or within one year after he has ceased to be a member.

This organisation would have the following advantages:—

1 Existing members could be asked, and new members compelled to become members of the Company. In this way membership of the Club and the Company would in due course be identical.

2 No cash would have to be subscribed by members on their becoming members of the Company.

3 As there would be no transferable shares, and only members of the Club would be eligible as members of the Company, there could be no possibility of the Company getting out of the hands of members of the Club, and no single group of members could gain control of the Company.

The Property to be acquired would be transferred to the Company Limited by guarantee, who would grant a Debenture for £12,000 upon the terms stated above to the present Company. As I have mentioned above, the repayments of capital will amount to £600 p.a. and the gross interest in the first year will amount to £720, thereafter it will decrease year by year.

I will now come to the question which I know will be in the minds of many of you. Is it going to cost the ordinary member any more? I can assure you that this question has been most carefully considered by your Committee, who are no more anxious to incur additional personal expense than anyone else. In our opinion it will not. This is not to say that subscriptions may not at some future time have to be increased, because the experience of the last few years has been that costs tend to rise, but there is no more reason why they should be increased if the Club becomes in effect a members Club than if it remains a proprietary Club, as at present. Indeed there is possibly less likelihood because there will be no shareholders to consider or provide for and the amount of the subscription will be decided by the members. We think it quite possible that entrance fees and green fees could, and perhaps should, be increased, but that is another matter.

The advantages to the members will, if this scheme is carried into effect be as follows:—

1 The control of the Club will be in the hands of the Members.

2 There will be no possibility of the ownership of the Course passing to outside persons.

3 Once the repayment instalments and interest have been set aside, any surplus funds can be used for the benefit of the Members. There will be no shareholders expecting dividends.

I will conclude this letter by saying that the scheme proposed has the blessing and support of the Board of Directors of the present Company. In his report for 1956 the Chairman said "... now that such a large proportion of shareholders do not live in this district and therefore are not in a position to take a proper interest in the Club and its future, I personally feel that efforts should be made to make Parkstone a Members' Club". If the scheme is approved by the Members of the Club, it will be placed before the shareholders of the Company for their approval, and the Board will recommend an acceptance.

Yours sincerely,
G. M. Iles
Captain

October 1960

P.S. Your attention is drawn to the point that this letter is addressed to Members of the Parkstone Golf Club only, and not to members of the Parkstone Ladies Golf Club who are not eligible to attend the meeting.

Dear Fellow Shareholders,

Proposed Members' Club

As this is such an important milestone in the history of Parkstone Golf Club Ltd., and the Club, I feel that some observations from your Chairman are called for.

In my first Report to Shareholders in 1956 I said, "Particularly now that such a large proportion of Shareholders do not live in this district and therefore are not in a position to take a proper interest in the Club and its future, I personally feel that efforts should be made to make Parkstone a Members' Club. However, this is a matter on which the Club must decide and the initiative must come from them. . . ."

In spite of many appeals, by past and present Boards, still only a regrettably small proportion of the Club Members are Shareholders. At one time, I understand, Committee Members had to be Shareholders. In efforts to make the shares more attractive the Company some years ago altered the Articles and also later turned the £1 shares into 4s. shares, hoping they would thus be more acceptable to Club Members.

I maintain a Club should, if possible, be owned and run by its Members, and not by a Public Company. Short of Members holding the shares, a Members' Club is the only way in which this can be brought about. I therefore strongly recommend the acceptance of the present proposals by shareholders. I will so vote in respect of my own holding, as will all the other Directors.

If you are unable to come to this meeting, please let me have your proxy in favour as per enclosed card.

Thanking you in anticipation and also for your valued support in the past,

Yours sincerely,

26th November, 1960

JOHN R. STUTT,

COMPANIES ACT 1948

PARKSTONE GOLF CLUB LIMITED

Notice is hereby given that an Extraordinary General Meeting of the Shareholders of the above named Company will be held at Parkstone Golf Club House on the 15th day of December at 3.30 p.m. for the purpose of considering and, if thought fit, passing the following Resolution, which will be proposed as an Ordinary Resolution.

RESOLUTION

(*a*) That the Company sell the Golf Course, 1 Building plot (with planning permission), Clubhouse, Accommodation Buildings, Goodwill, Furniture, Fittings and indoor and outdoor Equipment, all at the price of £12,000. Certain land between the 11th fairway and Shore Road, certain building sites, and the site of a proposed electricity sub-station between the 8th fairway and the road would be excluded from such sale. Fertiliser, &c., Stocks would be included.

(*b*) That the consumable stores in the Clubhouse be taken over at cost.

(*c*) That the Company leave the whole of the purchase money on loan, secured by a Debenture, repayable by yearly payments of not less than £600, with interest at 6% per annum on the balance for the time being outstanding.

(*d*) That the transaction be completed on the 1st January, 1961, or as soon as possible thereafter.

(*e*) That such other details and terms of sale that may arise, be left to be decided by the Board of Directors.

Dated this 28th day of November, 1960.

Registered Office:
St. Osmund's Road,
Parkstone,
Poole.

By order of the Board,
G. T. LAWSON,
Secretary.

NOTE: Shareholders who are unable to attend the Extraordinary General Meeting are requested to complete and return the enclosed form of proxy. Forms of proxy should be returned so as to reach the Company's registered office not later than forty-eight hours before the time fixed for the meeting.

The letter to shareholders and the resolution to sell the course to the members.

Parkstone Golf Club Limited

Directors:

J. R. STUTT, *Chairman*; A. J. BROOKS, *Vice-Chairman*; J. D. BOND; CMDR. G. H. BROWN, R.N.; G. HUMPHRIS; G. T. LAWSON; W. D. SIMMONDS, O.B.E.

Ladies and Gentlemen,

Proposed Members' Club

Earlier this year a request was made to the Board by the Committee of the Golf Club asking if they could have our assistance and co-operation in their aspirations to make Parkstone a Members' Club. Keeping in mind the desire of the Directors to help the Club in all possible ways, a scheme was drawn up, at a number of friendly meetings, to enable this to be brought about.

These proposals have since received the unanimous approval of Club Members in General Meeting and the Board are unanimous in recommending same to the Shareholders. The proposals will be submitted for your approval, according to the enclosed Resolution, at an Extraordinary Meeting called under the requirements of the Companies Act. This meeting will be held at the Golf Club House at 3.30 p.m. on the 15th December, 1960. For the benefit of Shareholders, particularly those living out of the district, the position may be outlined as follows.

Amongst the principal benefits which would result, if you approve of the change, is the elimination of dual control. When Club Committees do not have financial responsibility they can often make irresponsible proposals and demands. This dual control was the cause of trouble in the years before the war.

By owning their own club, Members will also have the pleasure of being able freely to assist and support it without feeling that they are only benefitting Shareholders, a very valuable consideration. Parkstone has a club spirit second to none and this proposed change should help it still further.

Another very important benefit is that there is a considerable saving in taxation, no income tax being levied on a Members' Club. In the last four years alone, your Company has paid over £2,000 in income tax.

The following is an excerpt from the Club Captain's recent letter on the subject to Members. This will no doubt be of interest to you. ". . . I should make it clear that we (the Committee) are not seeking to criticise the present Board, whose administration of the Club is, I think, excellent, nor do I wish to suggest that there has been any lack of goodwill between the Board and the Committee. It is obvious, however, that this happy state of affairs could very easily come to an end, as times change, and new personalities come on the scene. . . ."

It may be appropriate at this stage to recall that in 1927 the only way that funds could be raised to save the Course from builders was by forming a Public Company, with a suitable Prospectus. Eternal thanks are due, particularly to a number of larger Shareholders, who came to the rescue and put up the necessary capital to purchase, when the Club, as such, were unable to do so. If there had been no Shareholders there would have been no Course.

Since the formation of the Company, various attempts have been made by the Club to realise their ambition of a Members' Club but they have always failed, mainly on financial grounds.

Now that it has been proved that Parkstone can be run as an excellent going concern the main obstacle which deterred previous club committees has been removed. Parkstone Golf Club is now not only economically sound, but is also a splendid asset and one of Britain's great Golf Clubs.

At the Club's special request the Directors are glad to recommend helping them by loaning the Club the money to make the purchase, this loan would be secured by a Debenture.

The Board are very pleased therefore that it has been possible for them to assist in making the Club's ambition possible, particularly on very generous and workable terms. These terms, with the large reduction in the Capital, should assure the Club of a successful financial future. We feel sure, too, that Shareholders will also wish to give their blessing to the proposals.

It is proposed that your Company remain in being for the present. The Board would give careful consideration to the utilisation of the land remaining after the proposed sale of the Course and Clubhouse, etc. The Luscombe land, unfortunately, suffers from flooding due to the large amount of Council surface-water drainage emptying through it. Under an agreement, Poole Council are required to keep this system in working order, and action to enforce this is at present pending.

If the present proposals receive the sanction of Shareholders, it is the Board's intention to arrange for a return of capital. Details of this will be submitted with the Company's Annual Report next spring.

Provision will be made in the Agreement for the new Club to honour the trust undertaken by the Company in 1927 that a Golf Course be maintained on the site for all time.

Proxy Cards are enclosed for your use if you cannot attend the meeting.

26th November, 1960.

By order of the Board,

G. T. LAWSON,

Secretary.

Notice of the meeting to discuss the sale of the club.

3 *Ambitions achieved 1961 to 1986*

3 *Ambitions achieved 1961 to 1986*

The formative years

THERE WAS NO perceptible change in the character of the club following the membership take-over, but changes did occur gradually with the greater involvement of the members in the financial and general affairs of the club and in the social events which increased in number and variety. Prior to the change-over and probably throughout the history of the club the ambience was essentially that of a gentleman's club. The lounge was furnished with deep leather chairs and the members were drawn largely from retired officers of the armed forces, the colonial service, and from local professional people. The atmosphere was static and formal with no attempt to ease the discomfort of a newcomer, in fact the strategically placed chairs were regarded as being the private province of certain of the *old guard,* and christian names were seldom heard in conversation or in reference to other members.

The greatest change which has taken place in the post-war era, and which was accelerated by the new administration, was the broadening of the spectrum of membership and a dilution of the old system which had previously barred all but the titled and the professional classes. Prior to 1960 there were shareholders who were not eligible for membership. Bournemouth had always been populated mainly by the retired and the moderately wealthy, and there was very little indigenous industry to retain the younger element. However the trend towards increasing commercialism in Bournemouth and in Poole attracted a range of light industry which brought in skilled and unskilled work-people from all over the country, although mainly from the Midlands, and also enabled the local youth to find employment in their home area and to look for social and recreational outlets.

Junior members of the old club were few in number so it was not necessary to provide many special facilities for them, and because it was primarily a gentleman's social club, little effort

J Buchanan (seated) with G Kendall (plus fours), K Robshaw, Helen Ortwell and Sybil Kendall.

was made to encourage the progress of the young or to increase the standard of golf.

The character and the membership of the present club is therefore a microcosm of the great social and economic changes which have taken place in the area and in the country as a whole. Members demand high standards of accommodation and service, and on the golf course are deeply interested in the structure, maintenance, and the general conditions of play. The result of these changes is reflected in a far greater proportion of the club's finances being absorbed by course maintenance and staff costs; a constant upgrading of facilities within the clubhouse; and a comprehensive programme of entertainment which spans the calendar. In addition the membership reflects a total cross section of the population and social strata, and the club supports a thriving junior section whose needs and requirements are the responsibility of a specially selected member of the general committee.

The first committee to be appointed in 1961 consisted of James Buchanan, the captain and principal negotiator of the transfer of ownership, Geoffrey Iles the immediate past captain, George Kendall vice captain, Eric Nicholl treasurer, and Douglas Bond who agreed to continue as the club secretary, and ten other members. Their task was to encourage greater membership participation in the club's affairs, to increase the social usage of the clubhouse, and to generate increased income in order to repay the mortgage and to carry out the much needed improvements to the course and to the clubhouse.

The weather was no ally, the winter of 1962 was atrocious and the course was closed for three months. Snow was thick on the ground from Christmas until March and traffic was brought to a virtual standstill. Ken Robshaw compared the atmosphere in the clubhouse to that of a morgue, and he recalls that Calderwood the steward organised a punch party to which a surprising number of members turned up...clad in heavy overcoats and wellies, probably feeling grateful for an opportunity to see and talk to one another again. These Sunday punch parties became a popular weekly event and a number of people used the opportunity to cash cheques at the club...cheques which Douglas Bond did not present until after the weather cleared, with the result that a number of the regulars received a painful shock when their bank balances took a sudden nosedive. During this

One of the recipients of an electric wheelchair with some of the celebrities who supported the charity match.

l to r Eric Sykes, Richie Benaud, Toni Dalli and Jimmy Tarbuck.

period Peter Alliss erected a practice net in the starter's hut where he gave lessons and charged a shilling a session for the use of the net.

Fortunately such extremes of weather do not occur very frequently, but the loss of nearly three months' income must have been a severe blow to the new administration.

Charity events

The popularity of the course owed much to the successes of Peter Alliss who, when not playing tournaments, entertained many of the best-known professional golfers of the day and played in numerous pro-am and charity events on the course. Notable among the visiting professionals was Tony Lema who played in an exhibition match shortly before his tragic death in a plane crash.

Another popular charity event which gave the members a great deal of pleasure was the Lord Roberts Workshop appeal which featured (typically) Dai Rees, Bernard Hunt and Peter Alliss. The three would demonstrate trick shots from the edge of the first fairway, playing up the practice fairway of the old seventeenth. Dai Rees would press a ball into the surface with his foot then proceed to hit it well up the fairway with a four wood. Peter would pitch or chip shots into a green and Bernard Hunt would putt whilst Dai Rees would encourage the spectators to throw money on to the green. All this was backed up by raffles and auctions to amount to quite impressive contributions to the charity.

Prior to the sale of the club to its members Jack Stutt had bought a number of building plots from the company at the periphery of the course. At the time of the purchase the members bought back one of the plots alongside Compton Avenue near the junction with Lilliput Road for £4,400 for the purpose of creating an improved teeing area for the fifth. The fourth hole was a par three, which tended to create an irritating hold-up, so the copse near the green was removed and the green moved about forty yards to its present position. In addition the original tee which was perched high up on the hill behind the present teeing ground was abandoned. In an exhibition match with Peter Alliss, Tony Lema hit his tee shot to the centre of the new green and knocked in a ten yard putt for a two...Peter lost it with a birdie.

Before the course was rated as being too short for professional tournaments it was frequently used for the qualifying rounds of the *Martini* and *News of the World* events, and the *Strong's* tournament, which became known as *Peter's Benefit* because he won it so often. Dr Donald Holmes recalls playing with Peter in a practice round prior to the 1964 event when he played the first nine in twenty-seven, which included two four's, two two's and five three's. He particularly remembers Peter's drive on the sixth which reached the elbow near the bunker, from where he pitched to within inches of the pin. Needless to report he won the tournament again on the following day.

The course was a great favourite with the many show business personalities who appeared in Bournemouth. In the sixties the *Ha-Ho* society, which was formed by television personalities Peter Haigh and McDonald Hobley, staged many charity events and brought to the course the majority of the best-known entertainers of the day.

It has now become the fashion for visiting entertainers to apply for temporary membership for the duration of the Summer season. The late Dickie Henderson's well-known passion for golf made him a frequent visitor and he established firm friendships with a number of members. Max Bygraves has lived in the area for many years and has been a member since 1972.

Gordon Dean, a member who owns an estate agency business, has become well acquainted with the visiting show business people and can now be regarded as their local *accommodation and golfing agent.* The connection began when be found a flat for Bruce Forsythe's summer season in 1965 and the two of them played a lot of golf together. Gordon recalls one particularly funny incident when they were playing with Patrick Tallack, who was then only just beginning to make a name for himself as a golfing instructor. The head of Bruce's driver shot off when he drove from the elevated eighth tee, the ball just trickled to the edge of the tee, but the head flew about a hundred yards into the bog below and it took them about a quarter of an hour to find it.

On another occasion during one of the *Ha-Ho* events which included "007" Sean Connery, Gordon found his ten year old son making a minute examination of Connery's car, searching for the machine guns and the ejector seat controls.

Funny incidents involving show business people are usually carefully staged, but one genuine incident which occurred when Gordon was playing with Jimmy Tarbuck also illustrates how dry the course used to become before the irrigation system was improved. He and Tarbuck were overtaken on the first fairway by a young lad on roller skates! When questioned the boy innocently explained that he had been sent to fetch his dad for lunch.

The 1977 visit of Val Doonican saw the birth of the Parkstone connection with the *Golf Fanatics* society of sports and entertainment stars which aims to provide electric wheelchairs for

Dr. Norman Crow presenting Peter Alliss with a decorated bottle to commemorate his winning three Open Championships in a row... the Italian, Spanish and Portuguese; finishing with a score of 50 under fours in twelve rounds in three consecutive weeks.

crippled children. Gordon was asked if Parkstone would provide a team to raise money for a local child. The committee readily agreed and Gordon, who was the current club captain, raised a team from among the members and the show-biz people who were playing at Bournemouth. That first-ever event raised enough money to buy two chairs, which at that time cost about three hundred pounds each. It has since become a regular event, with the club donating the use of the course and each member of the team, which usually consists of about twenty-eight people a side, paying a match fee, which is augmented by various raffles and auctions. In nine years the event has raised over £8,000, which has been enough to buy nine chairs, and wherever possible these are given to local children. They are always presented before the match so that all who have contributed or given support can see the children and their families receiving the chairs from the stars.

Club characters

There is a separate chapter on the golfing achievements of some notable members, but the club has had its share of characters who have added spice to the golf and to the atmosphere in the clubhouse. Prominent was the secretary of the day, Douglas Bond; he had never learned to drive a car but, wearing a soft leather flying helmet of World War 1 vintage, he and his weaving bicycle constituted a real hazard on the local roads, a situation which was considerably worsened when he bought a motor scooter! Douglas was the *compleat diplomat* and never failed to greet and make welcome any newcomer to the clubhouse. He had served as a Paymaster in the Royal Navy and in 1915/16 was involved in designing a golf course near Scapa Flow for use by the officers serving in the Home Fleet. He was a man of many parts, and although he had only one eye, he played first class cricket for Gloucester. A funny story told about him during his time as secretary involved a cockerel which his wife kept with the backyard chickens. The bird appeared to be off colour and Douglas was instructed to take it to the vet. He stuck the hapless bird underneath his jacket and cycled to the surgery where he waited his turn, with the bird's head poking from his jacket...no doubt making complaining bird noises, much to the amusement of the other patients, because when it came his turn to go into the consulting room Douglas discovered that he had been waiting in the surgery of his own doctor.

George Kendall who was the club's treasurer for a number of years and the club captain in 1963, is remembered by the inscribed bar stool in the lounge, and on the course by a stand of pines which he planted in a defunct bunker which guarded the temporary twelfth green to the right of the present green. This is now known as *Kendall's copse* and is used as a sighting point for the drive from the twelfth tee.

A Marples, a contemporary member, was a survivor of the San Fransisco earthquake. He scored a hole-in-one at the age of ninety and is remembered for being able to read the *Financial Times* without the use of glasses. He gave up golf at the age of ninety-six so that he could concentrate on his invention of a hospital bed for paralysed patients...which he completed and which was demonstrated on television.

Hector King, the originator of Interflora, was a member in the 60s; and Jim Slane, the 1908 water polo Olympian, was a great character and a very popular member. He and Jack Stutt originated the *Ramblers*, a small society of retired members who played the local courses and met for a Christmas lunch every year, when the club president would be the guest speaker. He also organised the coach for members travelling to the away matches of the Hudson Trophy, in which the club were very successful in the sixties. This was a very well organised affair, complete with the steward who served the champagne and Guinness at the breakfast stop en route.

Another prominent member of the time exerted a considerable influence on the development of a number of young professional golfers who became household names in Britain. He was Edward Ernest Butten who lived in a house above the seventeenth green and who created the international organisation known as PA Management Consultants. He took up golf at the age of fifty-eight and within five years had achieved a handicap of six. He was determined to find a British golfer who could win the Open, and to this end he sponsored an initial group of four likely candidates, including Tommy Horton. They were subjected to a rigorous regime of coaching under the direction of Harry Weetman of the Selsdon Park club, but the strict routine led to the break-up of this first group, and the new recruits, which included Brian Barnes and under the direction of Max

Faulkner, soon succumbed to the same fate and the scheme was discontinued. Inevitably the Press labelled the young golfers *Butten Boys,* but they tended to be disparaging about the sponsor whom they suspected of pursuing ambitions of personal agrandisement...a suspicion roundly denied by all who knew him.

Gambling is always frowned upon in golf clubs, but it is impossible to entirely eliminate it, and the small stakes waged on the friendly fourballs have always been an integral part of the men's game. There are however instinctive and compulsive gamblers who cannot resist the temptation to add just a little more pressure to the game...usually in a good natured manner. A typical group in this category were David Garland Higgins, Roy Jenkins, John Clark, and Teddy Cotton the son of band-leader Billy Cotton. One of the numerous stories told about this group involves a bet during a fourball match in 1964 when Cotton challenged Roy Jenkins to drive the sixteenth with a putter. Naturally the wager was immediately and enthusiastically taken up, but one of the caddies also wanted to join in the betting. They were not willing to take money from a caddie, but it was agreed that he could take part on condition that if he lost he would have to carry all four sets of clubs back to the club-house. The putter proved to be adequate for the purpose and the luckless caddie was forced to stagger around with his heavy burden. The four usually started on the fifteenth so the poor man had a long hard day; it is to be hoped that he was suitably rewarded out of the proceeds of the wager.

Clubhouse modernisation

Just prior to the membership take-over the Board had planned to modernise and enlarge the clubhouse because the facilities had long become inadequate to meet the increasing needs, but they abandoned the idea when it became obvious that there might be a fundamental change in the management of the club. Many more members were using the clubhouse and it was becoming increasingly obvious that a major modernisation programme was needed. The old boardroom was being used as a dining room and the smoking room was in general use as a card-room and committee room, but the lounge was too small and the bar quickly became choked during social events. The resultant modernisation added a new shop for the professional, an extension to the lounge, improved changing facilities, and much-needed improvements to the stewards' quarters, but many members felt that the clubhouse would never be able to meet the changing demands, and that the only practical course was to build a purpose-designed clubhouse on another site. This was not the first time that such a drastic move had been suggested; John Clark's offer of the Forsyte Shades site in 1945 was rejected by the Board because of the fear of a loss of compensation under the Town and Country Planning Scheme. This time an elevated site quite close to the Forsyte Shades was being suggested and the building would have blended into the wooded hillside, in sharp contrast to the villa residence facade of the old clubhouse which, like its fellows, looked boldly out across the bay to proclaim the wealth and success of its owners.

A sub committee was appointed to investigate the practicality of the move and they produced a comprehensive report which compared the cost of updating the existing building with that of

This first major reconstruction of the clubhouse in 1976 added a secretary's office, an improved professional's shop and an enlarged lounge area.

moving to a new site. They estimated that the incorporation of a list of nine essential improvements would cost in the region of £46,000, but that the result would still fall short of the ideal, and in particular would not solve the old problem of inadequate car parking space, nor would it restore the views over the course which had become obscured over the years by the growth of the trees. The cost of building a new clubhouse on a site above the sixteenth tee they estimated as £88,000, and this they claimed would provide all the desired facilities plus adequate car parking as well as three convenient starting points and superb views over the course.

It was claimed that the sale of the clubhouse site, even including the possible repayment of the loss of building rights compensation, would have covered the cost of the new building, including clearing the site and making the car parks.

Prior to the extraordinary general meeting in Canford Cliffs village hall in March 1975 there appeared to be a substantial majority of members in favour of the move to a new site, but the objectors produced a cogent counter argument based on the opinion that it would not be possible to overcome the problem of mains drainage at the new site; the Council would not allow a busy junction to be opened on a dangerous bend in the Lilliput Road; and that there would be objections to the felling of the trees. The scheme would not be viable without planning permission to develop the site of the existing clubhouse, and the practice ground would become too remote, so that planning permission to develop this was also necessary, but that would incur the penalty of the repayment of the compensation for the loss of building rights which the company had received in 1959.

These objections were sufficient to turn the tide of opinion because when the proposal was put to the vote it was defeated by a majority of four to one. So once again the opportunity to acquire an elevated site with all the advantages of a purpose-built facility was lost, and yet another programme of clubhouse alterations was embarked upon, but these too proved to be inadequate because in 1986 the builders are again in possession. This time a much-needed extension of the ladies changing facilities is being installed which has necessitated moving the secretary's office from the front to the side of the building, and the problem of the bar *milling area* is again being tackled by cutting back the wall of the cardroom.

Course improvements

For the upkeep of the course the new greens committee decided to adhere to the practice of the Board by following the advice of a Reading based seed company, but in 1978, during the captaincy of Dr Donald Holmes, the committee consulted J A Arthur, a golf course agronomist who was retained by the R & A. He made a number of inspections during which he took core samples of the greens and fairways and recommended a course of correction which included upgrading the irrigation system and improving the aeration of the greens and fairways. The objective was to discourage the invasion of poor quality annual grasses and the re-establishment of firm, hard-wearing greens and fairways. His recommendations were controversial, but the committee acted on his advice, with the result that quite significant improvements were obtained; the irrigation system was upgraded, the drainage improved, and the routine management of the course was rigidly supervised. As described in the chapter which deals with the evolution of the course, drainage has always been a severe problem due to the building developments which have taken place around the course, and the practical problems associated with the outfall of the Luscombe stream.

There is little likelihood of finding a permanent solution to the drainage problem because of the boggy nature of the Luscombe valley, much of which is below sea level. The Luscombe stream is the main drainage channel for the course, but this now has to carry the added load of the surface water drainage from the roads on the Northern edge of the course, and the outfall is subject to tidal variations.

The lakes

The reservoir lakes, although not an integral part of the playing area, have always been put to good use by the members. In the early part of the club's history the larger lake was popular for boating and swimming, whilst the smaller one was often transformed into a skating rink. The water is fresh, although polluted by the Autumn leaf fall and by the millions of pine needles cast by the surrounding trees. The lakes have never been able to support fish life in spite of treatment to reduce the level of Alum which is a naturally occurring salt common to this area. Many attempts have been made to stock with trout, but the results have been disappointing. However, the latest experiment seems to be succeeding because there are signs that the carp which were introduced by Frank Spriggs in 1985 are thriving.

The water does however support abundant bird life. In addition to the inevitable gulls, moorhens and coot, there is a migrant population of mallard duck, and a family of Canada geese is produced regularly every Springtime, much to the delight of members and visitors. An intriguing aspect of this yearly event is that only one family of geese occupies the water. This is particularly surprising in view of the large population in the nearby Poole Park. Each year a contest is fought between two or three males, presumably descendants of the previous brood, for possession of the large lake, and in early Spring members are treated to the sight and sounds of a brood of six fluffy yellow goslings being shepherded around the edge of the water by the two wary parents. They grow at an amazing rate as they graze the surrounding fairways and soon take on the familiar brown and white coloration with the distinctive white collar and black neck. This year (1986) one of the brood developed a fault in the feather formation of one of its wings so that it is unable to fly. Its early efforts to follow the family taking off from the water evoked the sympathy of many members, but its loud honking seemed to express as much surprise as distress. It does not appear to be in any danger from the foxes which inhabit the course and it is noticeably fatter than the rest of the brood as a result of its sedentary life and the sympathetic feeding it receives from the householders bordering the reservoirs. It has become hand-tame and waits expectantly on the third and fifth tees because many of the lady members have taken to carrying tasty tidbits in their golf bags. In the Autumn the family of geese is joined by a solitary snow goose; a most unusual combination, but one which adds greatly to the lovely natural beauty of the golf course.

One of the pair of cottages adjacent to the old pumphouse has recently been demolished and it is understood that planning permission has been obtained for the eventual demolition of the other one and for the erection of a single larger house. This will end a link with the old waterworks which extends back well over a hundred years, and breaks the link with the club which has extended from 1910 when Lord Wimborne arranged to have the cottages and the pumphouse included in the contract of purchase in exchange for transferring to the Council the Ladies Walking Field in the centre of Poole.

This most recent clubhouse reconstruction, completed in 1987, has given the ladies a new and comprehensive changing facility. The secretary's office now overlooks the first fairway, and the bar and lounge areas have been opened up to provide improved access and panoramic views over the course.

4 *Evolution of the course*

4 *Evolution of the course*

THE LAND on which the course was built has been described elsewhere as a wilderness of trees and heather, so the aim of Lord Wimborne's land agents was to boost the value by clearing part of the area surrounding the defunct waterworks and constructing a golf course in order to promote an influx of wealthy gentlemen who would be encouraged to build their homes in close proximity to the course.

Prior to about 1880 little serious thought was given to the design or construction of golf courses; they usually evolved from a walk over a suitable area of sand dunes by a well-known golfer in the company of the promoters of the potential golf club. The golfer would suggest the sites for the holes and the recommended routes for reaching them, from teeing points which he favoured, based upon his prowess at the game. Little else would be done other than to clear away the worst of the rough to make *fair ways,* and to produce a reasonably smooth area around the hole by close-mowing the heather.

Nearly all of these early courses were constructed out of links land, which were strips of otherwise useless sandy heath which separated the sea from the cultivated land, but by the time Parkstone was hewn from the pinewoods, inland or park courses were becoming commonplace as the game increased in popularity.

These courses posed unique design problems, and a number of the more famous golfers of the day seized upon the opportunity to extend their earning capacity by designing or advising on the constructions of the new courses, where artificial contours and man-made hazards had to be introduced to emulate the classic links conditions.

Many of these early design efforts soon proved to be unsatisfactory and had to be drastically revamped; and it soon became apparent that very few of the famous golfers were able to convert their prowess at playing the game into creating the best conditions for it to be played.

Willie Park's design

The first of the true golf course designers was Willie Park Jnr; he had the flair, the imagination, and the dedication to match the golfing skills which made him the Open Champion in 1887 and '89. He is credited with designing the first layout of Sunningdale, which was later improved by Harry Colt, the secretary of the club, who later became a very well-known golf course architect.

Park devoted the last thirty years of his life to golf course design; he was responsible for Huntercombe, Broadstone, Coombe Hill, Formby, Gullane, Holinwell, Killarney, Worplesden and others in this country before going to America where he spent his later years designing over seventy golf courses in America and Canada.

There is no doubt therefore that Lord Wimborne chose the best designer, but there is evidence to suggest that severe pressures were exerted on Park to restrain his enthusiasm, and the area finally delineated for the course was restricted to a narrow peninsula at the western extremity, and excluded the two lakes, which would normally have been the focal point of any designer's plan. One possible explanation for this unfortunate exclusion is that the strip of land between the lakes and the road was more valuable as building land.

At the time of construction there was plenty of land available below the site of the clubhouse, which would have allowed the designer to include the larger lake in the plan, but the most convenient points of access to the course were from Parkstone station and from the tram stop at the top of St. Osmunds Road. There was a lane leading from the road, which eventually became Links Road, so it was obvious that the architect would wish to site the clubhouse at this point, and it would therefore follow that the immediate area would quickly become valuable building land, therefore the lakes had to be excluded.

Frank Gillett, who joined the groundstaff in 1919, became Head Greenkeeper and retired in 1967.

The *News of the World,* prominent in those days for its reporting and sponsoring of golf, described the course in a 1911 issue, just one year after the course was opened for play. The article mentioned some quite significant alterations which were being planned for the course, which tends to introduce some doubts as to the efficacy of Park's design. The reporter referred to great improvements being effected towards obviating the blind holes difficulty. For example, the shoulder of the hill at the second (now 3rd) was to be reduced and the spoil used to fill up a quarry hole to the right, *so that with a new tee behind a corner of the reservoir, a fine open and yet sporting drive is secured to the now four hundred yard hole. The sixth tee has been advanced twenty-five yards so that the hill may be carried by the drive, and a sight of the green obtained for the approach.*

As may be seen from the fold-out map, this hole has now disappeared, but it was roughly along the route of the seventh, although it measured 327 yards. The old seventh then carried on to a point roughly equal to the position of the present eleventh green.

The writer continued with observations on extensive alterations which were being carried out to the incoming half of the course. *The sixteenth hole is to be thrown into the seventeenth to make a fine two-shot dogleg of 400 yards. To effect this, two acres of tree-studded hillside have been cut away and the space turfed.* It can be seen from the same map that this made good sense but it again calls into question the validity of the original design.

It is interesting to note that the early 1920s landowner did not have to ask permission to cut down trees.

Another golfing correspondent, this time in 1927, described the course as having greens and fairways brought to a high level of perfection, and described it as *just about as attractive a golf course for the holiday golfer as could be imagined; there is not a colourless hole on the course, nor a corner of it that fails to fill the eye with its natural beauty.*

Further changes were made to the course following its purchase from Lord Wimborne and the installation of Reg Whitcombe as the Professional in 1928, but these were mostly of a cosmetic nature. The most intriguing aspects are the changes in the direction of the third, fourth and fifth holes, and the reduction of the sixth to a par three.

Braid's re-design

The most significant course improvement followed the purchase of the sixty-odd acres of marshland from Lord Alington in 1932, and the construction of the four new holes. The detail of this has been covered in Chapter 2, but this addition to the course, combined with the changes recommended by James Braid in his 1933 re-design, produced a course which is substantially that which is played today.

The new layout was officially opened in 1937, and fortunately *Golf Illustrated* accepted an invitation to send a representative, otherwise there would have been no record of the event. The short article is reproduced, but to make any sense it has to be read in conjunction with the fold-out map because the constant references to the old layout makes for tedious reading. In fact, the style of writing, which is somewhat pretentious, makes an interesting contrast with present-day sports journalism.

The Parkstone Golf Club have waited a long time to enjoy the changes to its course it sanctioned, but now they are accomplished facts I do think they have improved the course. For one thing, they have increased the length of the course by several hundred yards; for another, they have cut out most of the climbing that used to be such a trying feature for all but the young and very fit, so that now, although the course has been appreciably lengthened, the average player takes less time in which to play his round; and, finally, the new holes are an improvement from a golfing point of view over the holes they have superseded. James Braid was the architect, although his original design has been modified in many ways by the Parkstone committee, which believed, and I find myself in agreement with them, that Braid's original suggestions would have proved too difficult for the rank and file of golfers, who, after all, are the people who keep a golf club going.

The first hole is as it was, and this is followed by a new short second of 148 yards. It is a hole of which I am not particularly enamoured. It is in my opinion, just another short hole, the sort one finds on hundreds of courses up and down the country. ..... The new eighth (294 yds) is a well-bent affair to the left. From the teeing ground to the green, all the ground to the left is real no-man's land, and the player who hooks here will be very fortunate if he finds his ball, and perhaps more fortunate if he does not. On the right of the fairway there is a fringe of heather followed by bushes, and then an out-of-bounds road. The green defences are excellent, and there is a bunker on the fairway short of the green calculated to worry the good player. I am prepared to call this new eighth hole a good hole, but I do think it would be bettered if a little more room were allowed on the left.

For the new ninth (500 yds) I cannot find anything good to say. There is any amount of trouble on the right and the left for the wayward shot. .... When one does get a glimpse of the green it proves to be quite attractive in design and situation. But I do object to the extreme blindness of this hole. The good player going for his four, is faced with a blind tee shot and a blind second; the inferior player going for his five, is faced with a blind tee shot, a blind second, and very often a blind third. I believe Reggie Whitcombe says that at this hole in a medal round, he would never go for the green with his second; that is sufficient condemnation for me.

The tenth (396 yds) in spite of a most attractive and cleverly defended green, I disliked because the tee shot must be hit a good two hundred and fifty yards before a full view of the green can be obtained, and this I think is wrong in a hole of this length.

For the new eleventh (484 yds) I have practically nothing but praise. It calls for a long and well placed tee shot and an equally well placed second to attack a green bent away to the left and approached through a narrow opening between trees. If I have any criticism it is that I believe this hole would have been better if it had been thirty to fifty yards shorter. The second is, it is so difficult that it will persuade one to play more often for a five than one should. Nevertheless, it is a grand hole.

The new twelfth (344 yds), played back over the old eighth fairway towards the old eighth teeing ground, is, by the nature of the terrain, a three and a half. But it is contemplated putting down a new green to the right of the old twelfth fairway and short of the old eleventh teeing ground. This should be a great improvement since it will lengthen the hole and improve its shape. This will necessitate shifting the present thirteenth teeing ground to the old eleventh teeing ground, and then the new thirteenth, played to the old eleventh green, will be the old eleventh hole in its entirety.

The fourteenth is the old short ninth; the fifteenth the old tenth; and the present sixteenth is the old short thirteenth. (There seems to be some discrepancy here because the thirteenth on the old course was never a short hole).

For the new seventeenth (490 yds), one tees up to the right of the old fourteenth green and plays it to the old sixteenth green. This I think is the best hole on the course, calling for a long and accurately placed tee shot and a long and most accurately placed second. It remains too, a lovely hole for the inferior player, who must place his second meticulously to ease up his third.

The new eighteenth (230 yds) is, in my humble opinion, owing to a bunker situated hard up on the forefront of the green, almost impossible. If that bunker is to be left there, then the hole must be shortened to enable one to play it with an iron club. If one is asked to play it with wood, then the bunker must be taken away. At least that is how I see it. In every other particular it is a grand hole.

Present-day golfers of even mid-handicap rating will probably disagree with much of the criticism contained in this early appraisal of the revised course, but this only serves to demonstrate the truly remarkable improvements which have taken place in the development of golf balls and golf clubs. In addition, the standard of maintenance on the modern golf course has, with the improvements in golf equipment helped to shorten the distances by at least half a shot. For example, although the geography of the hole has been changed slightly since the article was written, the majority of mid-handicap players playing the par five ninth today would expect to have the green in sight for their third shot.

The war years

Like the majority of golf courses, Parkstone managed to keep going in spite of drastically reduced membership, reduced income, shortage of labour, fuel, and course maintenance. The Army moved in and set up a searchlight battery near the tenth green, which became a par three because of the huts which were built on the front half of the fairway, and only a small part of the green was available for use. Players then had to walk back along the edge of the fairway, cross the heath and the ditch, and play the eleventh from a small tee on the edge of the ditch. There was also an anti-aircraft gun emplacement near what is now the practice green at the back of the eighteenth tee, although this did not interfere with play.

The high ground around the eighth tee and fifteenth green was also in military hands, and the fifteenth green was encircled by barbed wire to keep the soldiers off the mown surface. Presumably there were local rules to give relief from the wire, but no records of this exist.

Many of the off-duty soldiers earned a few extra shillings caddying for the members, who were by definition, somewhat elderly, and some well-known sportsmen of the day but in drab service uniforms came to play; among them was Dick Burton the last Open winner before the war...he was then a Flying Officer in the RAF.

Many golf courses were ploughed up for food production, whilst others were spiked like hedgehogs to prevent the landing of enemy aircraft. Parkstone was spared these indignities; the thin acid soil is useless for food production, and the authorities, like many of the golfers, must have concluded that there was insufficient flat open space to tempt any but the most desperate airman to make a landing.

All round however were the scars of war. The whole of Sandbanks, and many parts of the coastline were taken over entirely by the armed forces, and Poole harbour was a major embarkation point for the D-day landings in June 1944.

The course did have a few trenches and gun points, and the Home Guard regularly patrolled the fairways and woods, playing out their own war games in readiness for the possibility of more serious encounters.

During the night air raids on Poole, decoy fires were sometimes lit on Brownsea Island, and it is said that a number of bombs actually fell on the course, fortunately without causing serious damage, except for destroying the roofs of the two cottages adjacent to the seventh tee. These were unoccupied at the time, but had previously been the homes of two members of the groundstaff. Following the damage, the cottages were allowed to fall into a state of serious deterioration, to such an extent that they were sold-off in 1949 as being beyond economic repair.

Early post-war years

This was a period of rehabilitation and rebuilding of the membership, which had been badly depleted by the war. But there was no lowering of standards; new applicants continued to be thoroughly vetted, and then, as now, Parkstone was one of the most sought-after clubs in the area. However, little was done to repair the course, except for the normal maintenance work, with the result that the general standard of the greens and fairways was to cause concern to the members for many years to come.

Attracted by what he had seen when he reconstructed the course in 1934, Jack Stutt moved in 1946 with his family from Scotland and settled into a house overlooking the seventeenth fairway. He developed an intense love for the course and sought to protect it against the possibility of a take-over and redevelopment as building land. From the time he joined the club in 1946 until the sale to the members in 1961, he accumulated a major shareholding in the company. When he was appointed to the Board in 1952, he overcame the opposition of many of his fellow board members to push through a comprehensive plan of course improvements designed to increase the depth and the quality of the topsoil and to change the nature of the greens, which, in his expert opinion, required re-seeding with grasses more suitable for modern usage. He became the Chairman of the Board in 1955, and this position obviously helped him in his campaign for increased expenditure on the course, but it must have been very difficult for the Board, in spite of their reluctance to spend the money, to ignore his expert arguments and obvious determination. It says a lot for his persuasive powers that in the years immediately following his appointment, the course upkeep costs more than doubled from the meagre average of £500 a year over the previous decade. Included in these costs were the lowering of the hill at the third; the construction of a new fourth green, and extending the hole to its present par-four length; lowering the fairway at the fifth to make the green more visible; lowering the hill at the ninth to make the second shot less blind; creating a new green at the twelfth and increasing the length of the hole; and the same at the thirteenth; raising the level area along the left-hand side of the fifteenth to stop balls running over into deep rough, and increasing the length of the hole by about eighty yards. At the seventeenth the left half of the hill in front of the tee was removed to give the handicap player a chance to reach level ground, so creating what is now affectionately called old man's alley. In addition to this considerable list of major improvements, many bumps and knobs were removed to facilitate mowing and rolling by machines, and much extra money was spent on soil dressings and course maintenance machinery.

During these various operations, which practically transformed the course, and raised it to a standard far above anything that had been achieved before, he loaned the club specialist machinery to enable the old concrete foundations left by the army to be lifted and removed, and a bulldozer to effect the major earth removal jobs.

Irrigation and drainage

In 1959, just before the transition to a members' club, it was decided to improve the irrigation system to cover the more vulnerable areas of the course such as the fifth, sixth, and fifteenth fairways, which were particularly susceptible to sunburn. Water was laid to the fairways and a great deal of effort was devoted to modifying and improving the design of the sprinkler heads to achieve a wider spread and a greater penetration of water. In addition, a number of travelling sprinklers were bought. These were a familiar sight on many golf courses at that time, they were mounted on small toothed wheels and were driven along by a crude hydraulic motor.

A fully automatic watering system had been installed in nine of the eighteen holes at the Denham (Bucks) golf course, and a full eighteen hole system at Handsworth in the Midlands. In 1960 Leslie Mileham, who was acting as the course supervisor, and Dick Peach, because of his wide engineering knowledge, inspected these installations, and in 1962 a similar system was bought by the club at a cost of £30,000. The system was installed by the British Ovehead Irrigation Ltd. (BOIL), and it consisted mainly of components from the American *TORO* system, with British adaptations. The installation was connected only to the greens, and for about ten years it was generally amended, modified and extended until, in 1979, an updated system costing £10,000 was put in. This in turn was superseded in 1982 by a new system which covered the greens, tees and fairways, and which incorporated the new large sprinklers with the oscillating heads, which are a feature of all the modern pop-up systems.

Before installing the new system, a new and more powerful pump was installed, and a new piped water supply, which was taken directly from the lake, because the Luscombe stream supply had become polluted by the surface water drainage from the surrounding roads.

The underground reservoirs below the pumphouse were drained and opened so that they could be inspected for possible damage and to check on the silt build-up. Dick Peach recalls how he viewed with awe the impressive cathedral-like caverns which had been constructed by the old water company. The two halls were lined with glazed yellow bricks, and except for some minor damage to the roofs caused by tree roots, the structure was in excellent condition and a great tribute to the skills of the Victorian builders. He estimated that the reservoirs could hold about three million gallons of water.

The natural drainage of the golf course has been materially affected over the years by the building operations, combined with the associated loss of trees, which have taken place adjacent to the course; and this, together with the increased influx of water into the Luscombe stream, has had serious effects on certain low-lying areas of the course. Between 1966 and 1971 nearly two miles of new drainage was installed, but the approach to the green at the ninth, and the eleventh fairway beyond the stream were prone to serious flooding, particularly at high tides. In spite of scepticism voiced by many of the members, Hamilton Stutt designed a scheme whereby the levels were raised with thousands of tons of sand which were taken from the hills beside the tenth and eleventh fairways, and this has considerably improved these local problems. Hamilton recalls that he had certain doubts of his own about the efficacy of the scheme, and as an insurance policy he made surreptitious enquiries about membership of Ferndown...fortunately the scheme worked very well!

A first for Parkstone which occurred at about this time was the purchase of the first triplex green mowers, which are now in universal use, but this was the first time the machine was seen in Europe.

The tenuous balance of water drainage which now exists will again be threatened by the development of the Compton Acres site alongside the fifteenth fairway.

The removal of trees and construction of service roads will undoubtedly add to the drainage problem which now affects the twelfth fairway which is close to sea level. A large number of trees and shrubs have already been planted along the boundary of the fifteenth, but it is doubtful if these measures will be adequate to compensate for the natural absorption of the original wooded site.

The general situation would be eased if the Poole Council would more readily comply with its obligation to maintain in good order the main drainage ditch and the outlet of the Luscombe stream which would allow the system to drain as the tide ebbed.

Course maintenance and improvements

Since 1970 the greens committee has carried out an intensive programme of woodland maintenance. This has been somewhat constrained by the Council's tree preservation policy, but it has been possible to maintain and sometimes improve the views of the lakes and the harbour from the various vantage points on the course, and in particular the views from the second, the eighth and the thirteenth tees. New medal tees have been constructed and existing ones enlarged at nine of the eighteen holes, and a new tee constructed between the lakes for the third hole. This is the only occasion that the water comes into play, and although the line to the hole is made somewhat easier from this tee, it is surprising what a psychological effect the water has, especially when one is carrying a medal card.

The lower car park is probably taken for granted by the majority of the present-day membership, but obtaining planning permission for its construction proved to be a long drawn-out affair. Its design was also fraught with much discussion, but the outcome is quite pleasing and retains much of the natural character of the land, and belies the problems of drainage and possible source of irritation to the local residents which occupied much of Hamilton Stutt's time throughout the design stage.

Many visitors to the course are intrigued by the presence of a green to the left of the seventeenth, which is now maintained as a pitch-and-putt practice area. This green was constructed in 1963 as part of an ambitious scheme to resite the hole and to clear the wooded heathland to the right of the present fairway in order to create a large practice area. The hole was to be shortened to a par four, played from the same tee and taken across at an angle to the left of the present fairway. The remainder of the fairway and the land to the right would have yielded sufficient ground which, when landscaped, would have provided excellent practice facilities. In the event the new green proved to be unpopular and was relegated to a practice green within a couple of years. The scheme to clear the wooded hillside was dropped because of the cost and because there was little hope of obtaining permission to fell the trees. If the plan to resite the clubhouse to the elevated area beside the sixteenth tee had materialised, then perhaps the plan to clear the ground to provide a much-needed practice area would have been pursued, but that is now mere conjecture.

The condition of the existing seventeenth green has been considerably improved by the removal of a number of the surrounding trees, which has allowed more light and ventilation to what was previously a dark and damp area. The only remaining problem is the wood ant which is particularly active on this green. As a species they are large and quite aggressive, so it is prudent to use the putter head to sweep them clear of the line!

As mentioned in the earlier chapter, a great deal of discussion took place between the Board of Directors and the members about the provision of a practice area. This was originally meant to be sited below the clubhouse, but that land has long since been sold and developed. No suitable alternative became available until after the final major reconstruction of the golf course in 1934 when the eighteenth hole was moved from the area now occupied by the bungalows near the entrance to the club. The seventeenth hole was resited at the same time and the old fairway was eventually used for the purpose and it has since been developed into the present practice area. Because of its triangular configuration the site is not ideal, but it has been considerably improved by the construction of a special tee and covered area for use by the professional, and by the installation of a specially made teeing ground across the width of the practice ground. This has added to the utility value and at the same time has tidied up what was previously a ragged boundary to the eighteenth fairway.

In addition to these improvements, the course surrounds were planted with hundreds of Rhododendron bushes and flowering deciduous trees, the entire stock of a bankrupted Hampshire nursery which was bought by Dr Donald Holmes in 1978 in order to balance the coniferous cover. More recently a scheme has been introduced and managed by Nick Cook, a current member and trustee of the club, to plant flowering shrubs and Spring bulbs to extend the period of colour provided by the Rhododendron and Broom through to late flowering Hydrangea, Lilac and Hebe. This scheme has been financed by contributions from the membership, and great care has been taken to ensure that the plantings have been outside the normal playing areas of the course so as not to interfere with the year-round course maintenance work.

The latest innovation has been the clearance of a large area of scrub adjacent to the ladies' eighth tee and the construction of a turf nursery. The first attempt to establish such a nursery failed due to lack of attention, but the need for turf replacement which does not have to rely on cutting the perimeters of fairways, should ensure a better result on this occasion. The cultivation of turf on this particular site is a final irony in the face of so much opposition to the purchase of this marshy land in the 1930s on the grounds that it could never be drained sufficiently to be suitable for golf. A far cry indeed from the World War 1 era when local people used to pick Sphagnum moss from the marsh for helping to heal cuts and other wounds. It is claimed that a great deal was sent to the old Cornelia hospital in Poole, and the emergency war-time hospital in the Mont Dore hotel in Bournemouth, which is now the Town Hall.

Esme Stuart-Smith presenting an illustrated plate to Captain Elwyn Davies on the occasion of the club's 75th anniversary. The occasion also marked Esme's retirement as secretary of the ladies club after thirteen years.

This modern view of the 1st should be compared with the photograph on page 24. The massive bunkers have disappeared... and so has the view over the lake to the bay.

Sylvan glade: this tranquil scene belies the controversy that Hamilton Stutt's design for the lower car park evoked among the local residents who feared possible noise and pollution.

The short 7th, rough and heather from tee to green.

Lovely view of the 1st green taken from the 18th tee.

View from the medal tee on the 3rd.

Putting on the 13th green with the 15th fairway in the background.

The Rowan alongside the forward tee visibly narrows the 11th where a good drive is necessary in order to clear the marsh and the open ditch.

The sweeping curve of the 13th with the deep bunker in front of the green.

5 *The Professionals*

5 *The Professionals*

THE PARKSTONE GOLF CLUB in its three phases over a period of seventy-six years has had only four professionals. Very little is known about the golfing prowess of the first one, either on his own course or on venues in the South-West. However, golfing ability was not the sole or even main consideration in the choice of professionals in the early nineteen hundreds. Clubmaking and an ability to teach and get along with the gentlemen members were the prime requirements, and in these aspects, and especially the former, **Hugh Williamson** was the ideal choice. In the view of the very few remaining members who knew him, he was a very polite and reserved person who was highly regarded as a clubmaker. He designed and patented a very advanced form of iron clubhead which was marketed nationwide, and which was similar in appearance to the modern sole-weighted design concept.

Reg Whitcombe was persuaded by the group of six businessmen who bought the club and course from Lord Wimborne to leave his brother at Came Down and to join the new proprietary club in 1928, and he brought with him his colleague Eddie LeSuer who also became a very well-known clubmaker. Reg spent his entire professional career at Parkstone in spite of receiving lucrative offers to entice him away after his Open Championship success in 1938.

Following the death of Whitcombe in 1956 **Peter Alliss** and his brother Alec moved from nearby Ferndown to take up their first professional appointment; with an arrangement which allowed Peter to parade his considerable talents on the world's golf circuit whilst Alec stayed at home to look after the shop. Moor Allerton beckoned in 1970 and Peter forsook the heather and the pines and shortly afterwards, following the death of his mentor Henry Longhurst, he entered a new career which was to win for him even greater recognition and reward.

Keith Hockey who was appointed in 1970 represents a completely different approach from his immediate predecessors; he has concentrated on the administrative aspects of the professional golf scene and on perfecting his teaching skills, which have been recognised by his peers in his appointment as chairman of the PGA; captaining a PGA team which twice beat the Americans; and by his appointment to the teaching panel of the PGA.

Jack Stutt and Roy Beckett presenting Rodney Davis with the cup for the 1986 Club Championship. Rod became the first Junior ever to win the event when he beat Roger Hearn in the final.

HUGH WILLIAMSON
1910 to 1927

The club's first Professional was born in Grantham, Lincs in 1881, the brother of Tom Williamson of the Holinwell (Notts) Golf Club, who is remembered for having coached Enid Wilson the three-times lady Open Champion.

The PGA records for the period show that Hugh's younger brother Edmund was elected to membership in 1913, and this indicates that he had become an Assistant at Parkstone, either in addition to, or as a replacement for Padley who was mentioned in early local newspaper reports.

Hugh Williamson did not feature in the golf reporting of the day, so it has to be assumed that he was not a successful tournament player, but like most of his contemporaries he was a skilful clubmaker. However he went further than most by designing and patenting an iron clubhead which was manufactured under the trade name *WEPATUM* by the Stadium Golf Company. The clubs were of advanced design and resembled the modern concept of sole-weighting, but the design proved to be impractical prior to the invention of the steel shaft, because its short socket imparted too much strain on the hickory shafts of the day.

It is known that he left Parkstone at the end of 1927 when the Directors appointed Reg Whitcombe, and in 1928 he went to the Dolder Grand Hotel in Zurich. This was the site of a nine hole golf course, the only course in Switzerland at the time. He won the Swiss Open in 1928, then helped his brother to create a full championship layout which became known as the Zurich Golf and Country Club, where he remained as the Professional until 1931.

He returned to England in 1932 and took over the licence of the Crown Hotel in Matlock, Derbyshire, but he did not stay for long, returning to Bournemouth, where in 1937 he ended his life in tragic circumstances.

REG WHITCOMBE
1928 to 1956

The younger of three brothers, Reg put the family name into the Open Championship record books when, in 1938, in atrocious conditions he conquered the Sandwich course, so making amends for the previous year, when, in a deluge, he lost to Henry Cotton. Ernest the elder brother came close to winning at Hoylake in 1924, and in 1934 Charles, the middle brother seemed to have the title in his hands, but lost to Perry.

All three were born in a house overlooking the Burnham and Berrow course, and in his book *Golf's No Mystery* Reg stated that his first club was a sand iron with a face no bigger than the old half-crown coin, which had been given to him by the great J H Taylor. In 1912 be became apprenticed to brother Ernest at Came Down, and after a brief spell in the Army, he worked single-handed on the course until the brothers were re-united after the War. He played his first competition at Westward Ho in 1921 and tore up his card in the second round, only to find that if he had handed it in, he would have finished second behind Ernest!

His record in the West of England Professional Championship, beginning in 1922 was so impressive that it could have been the reason why the Directors of the new Parkstone Golf Club Ltd. approached him to leave Came Down to join the club in place of Hugh Williamson.

He certainly helped to put Parkstone on the golfing map with his wonderful record in the home professional tournaments; he was rarely out of the news, and in 1935 with his appearance in the Ryder Cup team, he set a precedent which his successor Peter Alliss was to continue for nearly ten years.

One notable victory, which was talked about for many years afterwards, was the thirty-six hole challenge match which he played with Henry Cotton against Bobby Locke and Sid Brews for a stake of £500 at Walton Heath in 1938.

PETER ALLISS
1957 to 1970

Parkstone was Peter Alliss' first professional appointment, and he and brother Alec must have left the Ferndown club with a great deal of trepidation at the prospect of following such a great golfer, and a well-loved club member as Whitcombe.

He had demonstrated his golfing prowess in Continental Open Championships, and had made three out of nine appearances in the Canada Cup team but he had had no previous experience as a club professional.

The directors chose him from about one hundred and fifty applicants from all over Europe, and they planned for him to continue playing the golf circuits of the world, acting as an ambassador for the club, and for Alec to run the shop.

Shortly after Peter's arrival the club underwent its most important transition, and in the years that followed, his tournament successes helped to attract an increasing number of visitors, and in addition, he invited many fellow professionals to hold exhibition and charity matches on the course.

During the heyday of his golfing successes, Peter was described as having superb natural talents and a swing of classical grace and power, but in spite of such attributes, he never managed to win one of the recognised major honours. He did win a host of professional tournaments in Britain, and Open competitions in Europe, but only once did he manage to reach the semi-final of the Matchplay Championship. He also had a fine record in the Ryder Cup competition, and his appearances created a record in that he and father Percy were the only father and son on either side to have played in the competition.

Peter left Parkstone in 1970 to join Moor Allerton in Leeds, and is nowadays better known for his television appearances in *Around with Alliss.* He is also without doubt the best of the television golf commentators.

KEITH HOCKEY
1970 to date

When Henry Cotton replaced the legendary J H Taylor at the Royal Mid Surrey Golf Club he announced his intention of building up a team of professionals around himself, and as part of this process he engaged Keith as an Assistant at the age of sixteen.

After spending four years under the tutelage of Cotton Keith decided he would concentrate on the teaching and administrative side of the game in preference to the tournament aspect. He spent a year in Norway then returned to join Reg Knight at Wanstead prior to taking up his first full professional appointment at Muswell Hill in 1953.

Following Peter Alliss' departure in 1970 he was chosen from a large number of applicants for the Parkstone post, and in the same year, when the PGA school moved to Lilleshall, he was appointed to the training and teaching staff. He became the Chairman of the PGA in 1974 and was appointed to the similar post in the West Region of the PGA.

He was responsible for collating and producing the PGA training manual, and in conjunction with the Bournemouth Management Centre, produced a correspondence course for the PGA Diploma in Golf Management.

He enjoyed a memorable year in 1983 when, as captain of the PGA, he led the Great Britain and Ireland team to victory over the Americans at Muirfield and repeated the feat in the following year at Turnberry. This helped to establish him as a natural leader and tactician and he is the first man to captain two winning teams against the Americans.

Since his arrival at Parkstone the shop has been enlarged and modernised and he has established for himself an enviable reputation for teaching.

6 *Notable members and their achievements*

6 *Notable members and their achievements*

A COURSE which was designed by a winner of the Open golf championship and redesigned by another would surely breed one of its own, and so it proved when Reg Whitcombe donned the crown in 1938. He was followed by another great professional tournament player who went on to become even more famous as a television commentator; and who in turn was followed by a professional dedicated to the administrative side of golf; to coaching the young hopefuls, and twice captaining a PGA side which beat the Americans.

On the amateur side, the club produced Miss Phyllis Wade the 1934 English Ladies Champion; the first-ever Dorset Ladies Champion and County Captain; *the best-ever lady golfer to play out of Dorset;* and the only non-American woman to be awarded the Bobby Jones award *for distinguished sportsmanship in golf.*

The men have scored successes ranging from the English Amateur Championship to eighteen Dorset amatuer titles and three South Western titles. One scored two holes-in-one in a single round of a foursomes competition, and another was dubbed a *boy wonder* by the press when he played exhibition matches with three professionals at the age of fifteen. Ted Garrett won the Dorset men's championship at the age of twenty-one, and in 1971 won the Grand Challenge Cup at Royal St. George's with the same two scores that Jack Nicklaus carded when he won it as an amateur.

The young Garrett was a prodigious hitter of a golf ball, and on one occasion he hit twenty-six balls across the Thames with a five iron. The event was organised by the owner of a public house at Richmond who devised the scheme for charity. He asked Ted to desist because every ball which carried the river earned the player two free pints of beer, and the cost per shot was only 10p!

Eight of the men have represented the SW counties against the Midlands, which is regarded as being just a step away from international honours. They are Ernie Millward, Ken Longmore, Dick Peach, Roger Hearn, Roy Francis, John Gordon, Dr Donald Holmes and the eighteen year old Steven Edgeley.

Another most unusual record, perhaps unique in a club with such a short history, is the one held by the family of Esme Stuart-Smith. Beginning with Esme's father Capt. T Homer who played in the team which beat the professionals in the first recorded pro-am event in 1919, and who won the Wimborne Cup in 1920, the family has produced four generations of winners. Esme's impressive career spanned over fifty years and is dealt with in some detail in the following pages. Daughter Tessa won the Long Handicap Cup in 1983, the Bronze Trophy in '84 and the Dorset Bronze Championship in '86. Son Ted Hill won the Robshaw Cup in 1956 and was runner-up in the 1958 Dorset Boys Championship. The fourth generation is represented by Timothy Hill who won the same Robshaw trophy in 1984 and was also runner-up in the Dorset Boys Championship in the following year. He won the Rotary *Golfing for Youth* in '85 and was Parkstone's qualifier for *Golf World's Most Improved Golfer of the Year* when he reduced his handicap from 18 to 8. In 1986 he won the *Daily Telegraph Junior Golfer of the Year,* and his brother Nick won the under fifteen section of the Dorset Boys Championship in 1984.

Ernest Millward established a new course record in October 1947 and was involved in what was claimed to be a world record. In the 36-hole Wimborne Cup event he scored 67 in the morning round and holed his tee shot at the fourteenth. The ace was equalled by G H Crisp; and Greville Humphris holed his tee shot at the short second, making three aces and one course record in one event. In the afternoon round Millward scored 70 which gave him a winning total of 137.

It is also worth recording a remarkable *failure.* Ken Clarke, playing off a handicap of two, matched the Broadstone course record in the Summer of 1978 with a round of 66; he then scored 64 in the Parkstone club championship, which was one better than the existing record. Unfortunately records are only set on stroke play, so the 64 did not count. However, it was a remarkable feat, which included eight birdies, five on the last nine which he did in a five-under-par 30.

In the following pages are featured a few more of the many notable players the club has produced from the three phases of its history; from titled patronage through a turbulent period of company ownership and into the 1960s when the members bought the club and began to run it for themselves. There are so many fine achievements to choose from that it has been possible to include only the most outstanding personal successes.

Winners all. Esme Stuart-Smith (4th from l) with her daughter Tessa and son Ted, who with their sons Timothy and Nick made up three of the four generations of winners described in the preceding page.

E M S ARKELL (Arkie) was born in Bristol in 1895 and first took an interest in golf through caddying for her mother, and knocking balls from the kitchen garden into the paddock.

She is unable to recall the date or the level of her first handicap, but she became a member of Parkstone when her family moved to Canford Cliffs in 1917, and stayed until she moved to West Parley and joined Ferndown in 1945.

The County Association was formed in 1911 and disbanded due to the War in 1913, but in 1920 when it was reformed Arkie was on the first committee. She suggested the formation of the ladies' county championship in 1923; won it for the first two years, and again ten years later.

She was a member of the county team in the finals of 1930, '32 and '36, and won the LGU Challenge Bowl in 1924. She captained Dorset in 1953, '54 and '64, and was President of the County Golf Union from 1972 until 1976.

In 1931 she entered for the Swiss Open Championship at Lucerne and won the title after the organisers consented to change the date of the final in deference to Arkie's objection to playing on a Sunday.

At age sixty-nine she played in a foursomes match against a mens team drawn from county players and professionals.

An eye operation in 1982 put an end to her playing career but she remains a very keen follower of the game.

JEANNE BISGOOD won five European amateur titles; made eight appearances in the English national side; three in the Curtis Cup team; and two in the Vagliano Cup team. She was three times English Ladies Amateur Champion, won her native Surrey county title three times, and the Parkstone Ladies Championship eleven times. Small wonder that she has been described as the best lady golfer ever to have played out of Dorset.

She qualified as a Barrister, and practised from 1948 until 1953, but hit the headlines by beating the American champion Grace Lenscyk in the British Amateur Championship of 1949, and this won her a place in the British Isles side. Her Curtis Cup debut followed in 1950, the year she won the South-East title, a feat she was to repeat in 1952. That was a great year for Jeanne; the Curtis Cup team notched up their first-ever win over America, and she won the Astor Salver and the Roehampton Gold Cup for the second successive year... and topped it off by winning her first European title in the Swedish Open.

1953 brought her a hat-trick of victories in the Astor Salver and Roehampton Gold Cup; her second Surrey county title; a repeat of her 1951 victory in the English Ladies Championship; and the German and Italian titles.

By 1954 she had enjoyed an unbroken six-years in the English national team, and in that year made her third appearance in the Curtis Cup team. It was also the year that she won the Portuguese Ladies. In 1955 she added the Norwegian title, and in 1957 won the English Ladies for the third time. One major title eluded her — British Amateur; her best performance was at Broadstone in 1951, when she lost at the twenty-second hole to the eventual winner.

After her 1951 success in the English Ladies she was made an honorary member of Parkstone, so creating a unique hat-trick; her father was so honoured when he became the President of the club in 1948, and her mother in 1949.

PAT CROW played tennis as well as golf for Kent in 1938 and '39, playing to a handicap of four, then gave up playing golf for twelve years. She moved to Dorset in 1946 and joined Parkstone in 1951 and within a year she won the first of ten county titles.

Three consecutive titles fell to her in the '50s and '60s and she won the South-Western title twice, in 1954 and '55 only just failing to make it a hat-trick in 1961 when she was beaten by the international player Ruth Porter.

Pat played a lot of golf with Jeanne Bisgood, and lost to her in the quarter-finals of the English in the year Jeanne won the title at the Queens Park course in Bournemouth.

In 1978 Pat completed twenty-five years of competitive golf for Dorset, but her most memorable round was with Peter Alliss when they won the Broadstone Platters in 1961. She also partnered Dick Peach in county mixed foursome matches and they won numerous titles, including the one at Parkstone in 1961 when Dick holed-in-one twice in the same round.

On the administrative side, she was the LGU scratch representative for the South-West, and was President of the Dorset Ladies County Golf Union before she left Dorset in 1980 to live near her family in Perthshire.

Her late husband Norman was a popular member of Parkstone; a scratch player, he played for Cambridge in his university days.

Pat is now a member of Auchterarder and Gleneagles and still plays to a handicap of seven at the age of seventy. She has just recorded her seventh hole-in-one, on the seventeenth at Gleneagles.

BARBARA DIXON started to play golf at the age of eleven at Ashford Manor where she was encouraged by Jimmy Hitchcock to take the game seriously. This she did, to such effect that at fifteen she was chosen for the county second team, and it was at one of these matches that Maureen Garrett recommended her for LGU coaching by Syd Scot at Roehampton.

The family moved to Parkstone in 1963, and this was followed by selection for the county team, for whom she played for seven years; and successes in the County Championships in 1966, '68 and '70. During this time she was coached by Doug Sewell of Ferndown, and she reached the quarter-finals playing with him in the Sunningdale Foursomes in 1970.

1969 was *decision year* for Barbara, and what a decision it proved to be: she gave up her safe job in the bank so that she could spend a year on the circuit *to have a go and see if I could do anything.* After two months of hard practice, she started by winning the English Ladies Championship at Burnham and Berrow, beating Margaret Wenyan the Derbyshire champion by 6 & 4 with Jeanne Bisgood as her caddie. She holed practically everything from about twenty feet, using a putter that had been given to her by a friend eight years previously.

Following that victory she was selected to play for England in the European Team Championship in Sweden; was runner-up in the Wills Tournament; played in the home internationals (Western Gailes) and the Vagliano team in France; and was a semi-finalist in the Worplesden Mixed Foursomes, playing with Tony Richmond.

Marriage in 1970, and a change of name to McIntosh, meant a move to Scotland, but the successes continued with wins at the 1971 *Scottish Evening Times* Foursomes; the Avia Division 2 Ladies Foursomes in 1972; the East Lothian Championship in 1975; and Captain of her county team in 1985/86.

MAUREEN GARRETT's father was President of the County Golf Union for eleven years and President of the EGU in 1958, so it was perhaps fitting that Maureen should also make an impact on the game. But what an impact... she was runner-up for the Middlesex county title at the age of fifteen, and won it the following year; captained England to victory in three home internationals; twice reached the semi-finals in the British Championships; and in the early 1950s was, at plus three, the lowest handicapped lady golfer in Europe.

She was taught by Archie Compston at Coombe Hill, and was greatly encouraged by her father. She lived and went to school in London, but from the age of four until her marriage in 1948, she played her golf mainly at weekends and during the family holidays in Sandbanks. Maureen joined Parkstone in 1935 and set a course record for ladies in 1953 with a round of 69.

In 1947 she became the first British lady golfer to play in America after the War, where she reached two semi-finals and was feted everywhere she went. Maureen won the French Open in 1946 and played in her first Curtis Cup match two years later when the team lost to the Americans at Royal Birkdale. She captained the Curtis Cup team in 1960, and the Great Britain team against the Continent of Europe in 1959, and played for England four times between 1947 and '53.

A contemporary of Jeanne Bisgood, the pair were a formidable force in British golf and romped away with the scratch and handicap titles in the second division of the Avia Foursomes at the Berkshire in 1979.

In 1982 Maureen crowned her illustrious career when she was appointed President of the LGU and was honoured in America with the Bobby Jones award for distinguished sportsmanship in golf, the first non-American woman to be so honoured and only the sixth women ever to have achieved the distinction.

ESME STUART-SMITH received her golf tuition from Ernie Whitcombe who insisted that until she gained a single-figure handicap she should learn to *manufacture* shots by playing with a half-set of clubs.

In 1928 she left school and joined the Bournemouth club at Meyrick Park, where her father was a scratch player. Dedication, and Whitcombe's tuition soon paid off because she won the first competition she ever entered... and had her thirty-six handicap reduced to twenty-seven.

She reached her single-figure goal in the early thirties, and became a member of the Hampshire ladies team (presumably with a full set of clubs), and by 1938 was playing consistently to a two handicap. However, the war and the impending birth of her first child put a temporary stop to competitive golf.

After the war, and now a member of Parkstone, Esme won the Dorset Ladies Championship in 1948, '51, '58 and '65, and also won the Parkstone Ladies Championship four times. She twice reached the final of the South West Championship, and also played in the Open and the English Championships, *but only if they did not involve too much travelling.*

She scored four holes-in-one, three at Parkstone, and one particularly satisfying one during a County match at High Post.

Her record on the administrative side has been equally impressive: County captain three times; Vice Chairman of the English Golf Association in 1974 and Chairman in 1975; Captain of Parkstone ladies four times, and secretary of the ladies club for thirteen years until her retirement in 1985.

Esme's most memorable golfing achievement was at Hunstanton in the British Championship of 1946 when she beat the favourite at the twenty-first hole, *but the next round was a bit of an anti-climax* she admitted ruefully.

In recognition of her golfing achievements and her services to the Parkstone club, Esme was made an honorary life member in 1976.

JANE SUGDEN's love of golf and her impressive record of achievements are disarmingly dismissed by such responses as *its a game like any other, and there are more important things in life than games.* Her record however belies such a dismissive attitude, because such success cannot be gained without practice, dedication, and considerable talent.

Jane comes from a sporting family: her father Rex Machin played cricket for Cambridge in his youth, then kept wicket for Surrey. On school holidays in St. Enodoc, Jane would play with her mother and father, both of whom were very good golfers; She played with her father in the Worplesden Foursomes, and with her husband John; then in 1976 reached the semi-final of the Family Foursomes at Burhill with her son Christopher.

After leaving school and completing a secretarial course, Jane was fortunate to get a job which allowed her to practice on most days. She was coached by Norman Roffe the Professional at Finham in Coventry, and it was there that she met and made friends with Pam Davies (later Pam Large) who was to become her arch rival in the Midland Division of the LGU.

In 1951 she was a finalist in the Warwickshire County Championship; reached the semi-final in the Benelux Championship in 1953; and the semi-final of the English Close Championship in the following year. In 1968 and again in 1972 she won the Northamptonshire County Championship, and took the Dorset title four times... in 1964, '75, '76 and '83. She became the champion of Parkstone twice; in 1961 and '77.

Appearances in a British team which toured Scandinavia in 1952 were followed by a place in the England team against Canadian and New Zealand teams in 1953. She was also a member of the English home international team for three consecutive years from 1953, and she is currently the scratch score representative for the South West, and an English selector.

The pursuit of a good golf swing and a single-figure handicap has attracted many famous personalities from cricket, football, boxing and the entertainment world, and they have become almost as famous in their new pursuit as in their own professions, but there are not many *speedway riders* among them.

One exception is **BRIAN CRUTCHER** who began his career with the Poole Pirates at the age of fifteen, and retired ten years later as the number one in the British speedway world. He moved from Poole to the Wembley Lions in 1953, and was the number one rider in the team until its dissolution in 1956. For the next four years he rode for the Southampton Saints and made his last appearance at Oxford in May 1960. In that ten years he won every major prize in the sport except the world championship. He was British Match Race Champion for three years; runner-up in the 1954 world championship at the age of eighteen; and captained the English team for six years.

He joined Parkstone a year before his last ride, and was taught to play by Cyril Hannam, a one-handicap member of the Artisan club. He was then tutored by John Stirling at Meyrick Park, and within a year was playing to a sixteen handicap, and by 1976 had reached his single-figure goal.

He won the Wimborne Cup in 1976 and has been a finalist in six club championships. He captained Dorset in 1984 and '85, and won the Variety Club of Great Britain matchplay championship in 1984.

Brian does not stand out in a crowd, being only five feet five inches in height, but his most outstanding attribute is his determination. His total commitment to an objective is reflected in the success he has achieved in the three main pursuits in his life: speedway; his motor sales business; and golf. He is in every sense a *professional,* and plays to win... irrespective of the odds. His nickname *Bumble* is attributed to John Stirling and relates to his quick-fire murmuring speech and habit of hitting the ball hard along the ground.

KEN LONGMORE had to contend with a *boy wonder* tag when, at the age of fifteen, he partnered Don Curtis the Professional at Queens Park in a series of eight exhibition matches against Reg Whitcombe and S H Vine... and they won every game. He became a scratch golfer at twenty and was plus one from 1948 until 1960.

Ken's record in county golf is phenomenal; he made his first appearance for Hampshire at nineteen and played for three years before switching to Dorset in 1946 and winning the county championship at Parkstone. He joined the club three years later and won the county title four times, being runner-up on six occasions between 1947 and 1960, and won the West of England Amateur Championship at Parkstone in 1960. His name appears on the Wimborne Cup for a record seven times and he has won the scratch medal and the club championship eight times.

He played in eighteen South-Western Championships, but the nearest he came to winning the title was in 1951 when he was runner-up to clubmate Ernie Millward the Walker Cup player. Ken had a trial for the Walker Cup team but his nerves let him down and he never won an international cap.

Ken captained the Dorset team in 1971 and '72 and was elected to the English Golf Union in 1972, following which he served on the Executive Committee for five years. He is still on the council of the EGU; has been President of the SW counties; and Captain of the SW counties team.

He is closely associated with junior golf in the county, and has been the junior delegate for Dorset and the SW counties since 1970. He has also been President of the Dorset County Golf Union and has served on the Golf Foundation for six years.

ERNEST MILLWARD was probably the best Dorset amateur male golfer. He won the SW counties championship in 1948, '51 and '52, the West of England championship in '50, '52 and '54, and was an English International from 1949 to '55. The climax of his career was the English championship which he won at Burnham and Berrow in 1952.

His list of successes included runner-up in the Brabazon Trophy; the British Amateur stroke-play championship in 1949, and a four times winner of the Wimborne Cup. He won the Dorset championship in 1948, '50 and '51 and was a regular Dorset and SW player from 1946 until '57. His successes at Parkstone included the club championship in 1951 and '58; the scratch medal in 1948, '49, and '50, and his amateur course record of 67 in the Wimborne Cup has not yet been equalled.

He was regarded by many as a *rough diamond,* and he could be rather outspoken, especially with the traditional golfing establishment, but those who knew him well regarded him as a kind and loyal friend. His hobby, apart from golf, was restoring wrecked sports cars, usually the Jaguar XK 120. Throughout his time at Parkstone, from 1947 until 1958, he held a handicap of scratch or plus one, but he was always pleased to play with a high handicap player if drawn with him in a club competition, and would be at pains to put him at ease.

Like so many physically strong men, he was not a long hitter, but had a most delicate putting touch, and few could equal his prowess with a wedge. During his brief playing career he would practice hard for several hours a day, but when financial pressures intervened, he gave up the game intending to return to it later. Unfortunately this was not to be, because in January 1966, when called out in the night to a gang of youths in a car who were causing a disturbance at the Ossemsley Manor Country Club which he then owned, he was run over by the youths and killed.

ERIC NICHOLL started to play golf at twelve years of age, during school holidays with his father. He did not receive any formal tuition, but copied the methods of such legendary idols as Vardon, Bobby Jones and Abe Mitchell... to such good effect that when he joined the Bradford club of West Bowling at the age of twelve, his handicap matched his age, and he whittled this down to scratch by the time he was twenty-eight.

He was made captain of the club; played for the Yorkshire county side; and reached the semi-final of the county championship; and won the Bradford and District championship in 1932.

Eric moved to Dorset in 1935 and in the following year won the Bournemouth 36-hole scratch competition at Queens Park with an aggregate score of 148 (77 & 71). His first attempt at the Dorset championship ended after nine holes when the Came Down course became enveloped in sea fog, but he won it at Broadstone in 1938.

He was a regular member of the Dorset team between 1947 and 1955, and captained the team which won the South Western Counties Championship at Burnham and Berrow in 1954.

Apart from handicap events, his main successes at Parkstone were three times winner of both the scratch medal and the club championship. He was made captain of the club in 1950, and during the change-over of the club ownership in 1960, he was one of the three trustees of the new club.

During his sixty years of playing golf he has scored fifteen holes-in-one, the last in 1979 at the sixteenth. When interviewed for this article Eric ruefully observed that finding the green is just as elusive as finding the hole these days!

DICK PEACH was introduced to golf at the age of seven when his father gave him four clubs specially made by the Professional at Cardross near Dumbarton.

He moved to Poole and joined Parkstone in 1946. In the following year he was selected for the county side and played frequently for the next twenty-five years.

He lost the County finals on three occasions, but also won it twice; in 1966 at Yeovil, and in 1968 at Broadstone.

In the Championships he tied at Broadstone in 1955, and lost the play-off; but won it the following year at St. Enodoc, setting up a course record of sixty-nine in the process.

He played for the S W Counties against Midlands Counties on several occasions, and in 1956 at Burnham beat John Beharrel the reigning British Amateur Champion, and with his Somerset partner Neville Jutsum, beat Beharrel and Roger Bayliss in the foursomes.

He captained Dorset for four years; served as President of the county association for nine years; and represented the county on the Council of the English Golf Union for a number of years, part of the time serving on the Executive Committee representing the South West Counties Golf Association.

He captained Parkstone in 1958 and '59, and won the club championship twice; the first time (1955) he beat Ernest Millward two-up after starting with five successive birdies. At the tenth, and two-up, he was six under par, and the remaining twenty-six holes proved to be a dog-fight at around par figures.

With such illustrious lady players as Barbara Dixon, Josie Cooper and Pat Crow, he won the mixed fours, on one famous occasion, holing out for one twice in the same round. He also partnered Alec Alliss to victory in the Am-Pro Foursomes (then the Flag Foursomes), and he and Nick Cook won the men's foursomes at Knighton Heath when it became a thirty-six hole medal event. In 1960 partnering Peter Alliss, he won the thirty-six hole medal Beaconsfield Foursomes.

JACK SANTALL was a *natural;* an ex-professional ice skater, he did not take up golf until he was twenty-six, but within a month of joining Parkstone in 1935 he was given a handicap of six, and in the following year was good enough to enter the English Amateur Championship at Deal. Within twelve months he was playing for Dorset county and was in the team in the last South-Western Championship meeting before the War.

Jack won the county title at forty-one, beating Philip Urlwin-Smith 4 & 3 at Ferndown, and a few months before his seventy-first birthday he won the club's scratch competition without once three-putting over the entire thirty-six holes. He beat Brian Crutcher by 4 & 3 and was quoted at the time as remarking *I don't know who was more pleased, Brian or I... he's a great sportsman.*

He was a big man in every sense of the word, and at six foot and fourteen stone, could hit the ball tremendous distances; at Barton-on-Sea for example, he drove his tee shot through the green at the 385 yard first hole, and on the same course he put a drive and a four iron through the green at the 605 yard twelfth.

In an interview in 1984 he recalled his second appearance in the English Amateur Championship when he played against Cyril Tolley at Saunton in 1937, *everyone told me that he could really hit a ball, but I managed to hit it about twenty or thirty yards past him at every hole... not that it did me any good because I got a good thrashing that day.*

Jack left Parkstone for Queens Park in 1962 and died in 1986.

BILL SHANKLAND is unique: capped in Australia's Rugby Union team of 1926, and the Rugby League tour of England in 1928; golf professional at twenty-seven; *in the frame* twice out of five appearances in the Open Championship; and helping to raise at least a quarter of a million pounds for charity in exhibition matches.

He retired from Potters Bar when he was sixty-five; was welcomed at Parkstone, and offered social membership with the courtesy of the course.

There is space for only the briefest outline of his crowded life, which began in Sydney in 1907. Rugby caps against South Africa, New Zealand and England set the course of his future career in sport. During the 1928 tour of England he resisted offers from Wigan and Leeds, but eventually joined Warrington, where he stayed for eight years and made three appearances in Wembley finals. On one occasion he was quizzed about his prowess at golf by the Prince of Wales.

Golf had always been a conflicting passion, and it finally transcended the field game in 1931, when, although still a professional rugby player, he was taken on as an Assistant by Bob Kenyon at West Lancs. A move to Haydock Park followed and then in 1938 he severed his connection with Warrington and moved to Templenewsum, succeeding Percy Alliss who moved to Beaconsfield, then in 1950 he moved to Potters Bar.

He played his first Open in 1937, and in 1939 came third after three-putting three of the last four holes. In the 1947 Open he again finished third, two shots behind the winner Fred Daly.

Between 1941 and '51 he played in over four hundred exhibition matches with Cotton, Bobby Locke, the Whitcombe brothers, Peter Thompson, Von Nida and Dai Rees, and entertainers Sid Field, Bud Flanagan, Dickie Henderson and Donald Peers, to raise money for charities.

Among his Assistants at Potters Bar was Tony Jacklin, who must owe much of his later success to the advice and training he received at Bill's hands.

7 *Presidents of the club*

7 *Presidents of the club*

THERE HAVE BEEN seven presidents since the club's inception, two of whom were the Lords Wimborne.

Ivor Bertie, first Baron of Canford Magna, owned the land and had the course constructed after the purchase of the water company's installations in 1909. He was married to Lady Cornelia Spencer-Churchill daughter of the seventh Duke of Marlborough. He died in February 1914 and was succeeded by his eldest son **Ivor Churchill,** the second Baron and the first Viscount, who was president at the time of the sale to the six businessmen in 1927, although it is not known how much interest he took in the activities of the club.

T W Simpson, the owner of Compton Acres which overlooked the fifteenth fairway, was elected the first president of the proprietary club in 1928 in recognition of his financial assistance in providing a loan of £7,500 to make up the balance of the £20,000 required to buy the course from Lord Wimborne.

Simpson reputedly made his fortune in Malaya, but he is best known for creating the famous Compton Acres gardens. He bought the mansion in 1920 and with his friend Ben Boothby conceived the idea of surrounding it with a unique series of separate independent gardens, so planned that only one garden could be seen at one time. Rather unkindly he is described in a local paper as being a wealthy philanthropist suffering from boredom and an unhappy marriage! Following his death in 1947, the Chairman of the Board of Directors, **Walter Shortt** a

Barrister living at *Uplands* in Parkstone was elected to replace him.

Shortt was the driving force behind the efforts to raise money to buy the course from Lord Wimborne to save the land from building development, and he was chiefly responsible for fending-off the many attempts from within and from outside bodies to sell-off the club. He will be best remembered for buying the Alington land in 1932 which allowed the course to be lengthened and reconstructed to its present format.

Shortt died in 1949, but he had resigned his position on the Board due to ill-health, and **Bertram Bisgood** was invited to be President of the club. He had provided valuable legal advice to the Board over many years and was an early supporter of member-ownership. He remained as President until his death in 1968 and was succeeded by **Jack Stutt,** whose appointment recognised the debt owed to him for facilitating the sale of the club to its members. Unfortunately failing health forced him to resign in 1976 and **Ken Robshaw,** who had joined the club in 1948 and had been intimately involved in the negotiations which led to the purchase by the members, was appointed... and remains as a most popular and much-loved member, renowned for his intriguing *nodding dog* putting action.

B L BISGOOD
1949 to 1969

Born in Glastonbury in 1881, the youngest of eleven children of John Bisgood, a former Royal Irish Constabulary Officer who became Deputy Chief Constable of Somerset.

He moved to London at seventeen and after qualifying as a solicitor, practised in the City until 1915. Sport dominated his spare time and he played cricket for Somerset, badminton for Ireland, hockey for Richmond and lawn tennis for Kew.

After serving in the Royal Artillery in the First World War, he became a member of the London Stock Exchange, where with one of his brothers he established the firm of jobbers which became Bisgood Bishop (now County Bisgood), and in 1922 married Dorothy Harvey (née Cundall) an all-England badminton champion and Wimbledon tennis player.

He retired in 1931 and after moving to Branksome Park, joined Parkstone, where he played regularly and became a familiar figure in the club. He was particularly anxious to see the ownership of the club pass to the membership, and at shareholders' meetings over the years he urged the company to help facilitate such a change. Simultaneously he encouraged successive club captains and committees to pursue the objective.

He was elected President of the County Ladies in 1955 and regularly attended the championships and county matches, but towards his eightieth birthday he developed arthritis in his hands and could no longer play. However he spent hours on the putting green, even when he was forced to use a walking frame. He went to the clubhouse nearly every day to have tea and to play bridge, until late 1967 when he became confined to a wheelchair, but even then, when there were four strong men available, he loved to be taken to the club.

He died in July 1968 in his eighty-eighth year.

J R STUTT
1969 to 1976

Born in 1897 in Paisley, the eldest in a family of five, Jack was left fatherless at the age of seventeen, and at the beginning of the Great War found himself as head of the family with his mother and four brothers and sisters to support.

After war service with the artillery during which most of his contemporaries were killed, he returned to found a sports ground and golf course company which was to become one of the largest in the country. By the time the next war began he had been involved in the construction or revision of eighty-two golf courses, often collaborating with James Braid, whom he met in 1923. Among his most memorable achievements were the remodelling of Carnoustie Open Championship course, and the landscaping of the British Empire Exhibition in 1936, for which he was presented to King George VI.

Jack married in 1924 and had one son, Hamilton, who entered the family business after University and war service in the RAF. The family moved from Scotland in 1946 and bought a house overlooking the seventeenth fairway, and one of their first actions was to join the golf club.

Although he started to play golf late in life, Jack won an impressive number of trophies including the Captains prize, but his fondest memory is that of founding the *Ramblers,* a group of senior members who met regularly and played in a spirit of good fellowship at Parkstone and many other courses.

Jack's wife Laura died in 1973 and he later met and married Geraldine Sayer, a member of the club who became the Lady Captain in 1980.

K V ROBSHAW
1976 to date

Born in Bishops Stortford, Herts in 1912, Ken was the youngest son in a family of five and when he was three months old the family moved to London. After the First World War they moved to Whitstable where he received most of his education. He began to learn golf at the age of eleven at the Seasalter golf club where Wanda Morgan was the star player. She won the British Ladies Championship in 1910 and played in the Curtis Cup on three occasions in the 1930s. Another well-known amateur at the club was Bernard Walsh whose father owned a small oyster shop in Whitstable and who eventually became the owner of the famous chain of Wheelers Restaurants in London.

After a period of working in Selfridges store Ken and his brother started a small electrical business in Folkestone in 1938. They developed the business into quite a sizeable radio and electrical distribution company with depots along the South coast and in 1976 sold it to the electrical giant Philips.

During an enforced stay in the Victoria Hospital in Folkestone Ken met and married his nurse Winifred, who is also a golfer and a member at Parkstone and they have three children. He moved to Parkstone in 1942 and joined the club in '48 where, he recalls, there used to be a permanent starter, and the hut on the first tee used to be connected to the secretary's office by a field telephone.

He was appointed captain of the club in 1956 and again in 1967. The lowest handicap he achieved was four and he featured in three club championship finals, but without success. He won the Wimborne Cup in 1958 and has scored eight holes-in-one, all at Parkstone. He became captain of the Radio Industries Golfing Society in 1960 and its President in 1962. In 1985 he was appointed the President of the Dorset County Golf Union.

FFS AVE
COMPTON
ACRES
AIRWAYS
LILLIPUT ROAD
BINGHAM AVENUE

OURSE